Don't Tread on US!

Signs of a 21st Century Political Awakening

WND Books

For J.F.

Without thinking too much about it in specific terms, I was showing the America I knew and observed to others who might not have noticed. My fundamental purpose is to interpret the typical American. I am a story teller.

— Norman Rockwell

Foreword

Samuel Adams, a leader in the Boston Tea Party and signer of the Declaration of Independence, declared at the State House in Philadelphia on August 1, 1776, *"Our contest is not only whether we ourselves shall be free, but whether there shall be left to mankind an asylum on earth for civil and religious liberty."*

The Revolutionists' fight for a haven for freedom has come full circle.

The tyranny of government and excessive taxes has once again trespassed over the lap of liberty.

Political positioning has trumped the power of the people.

The Constitution has been ousted by cash.

The Bill of Rights has been bartered for corporate bonuses.

And while fewer and fewer cries of injustice echo in the corridors of Congress, patriots' blood is bubbling to a boil from sea to shining sea.

Those bubbles have burst on the American scene, from the blogosphere to town halls, tea parties, and Washington marches. And this book represents those poignant patriotic moments captured for all of us to see.

Far more than mere memorials, they are inspirational illustrations. But whether or not they serve as catalysts for future freedom fights or dust collectors on coffee tables across the country depends solely upon the beholder.

Indeed, that's the challenge I pose to all who hold this book in their hands: to ponder the purpose of these patriotic rallies, to consider the costs of their causes and to pass on the principles of their pledges.

Some say we patriots are temporary pains on the political scene—that our passions are fleeting fires. But I know fighters. And we are like those who ignited the light of liberty at America's inception. We are those who weather the storms of oppression and who can persevere until we triumph over tyranny.

Of course, temptation will try many souls.

Discouragement will give way to depression and dormancy in many. And others will retreat at the sight of what appear to be overwhelming obstacles.

I remember often feeling that way as a young man in the hundreds of competitions I fought on my journey to become six-time, world middle-weight karate champion.

But any warrior (cultural or otherwise) will tell you that if you're going to slay the dragons, you have to adjust to a certain level of fear and intimidation. You have to find a certain level of comfort in staring down the impossible—in facing giants, often alone. There will be no victory without it.

No one typified this type of confrontational courage better than General George Washington and the Continental Army, especially as they endured the winter at Valley Forge. They modeled for us how we must be, as we face our own wintry valleys.

There are no promises at the moment. No visions of

grandeur. Just some battle-scarred and wearied soldiers living in what our enemies consider tattered extremist huts made of straw.

These are long nights of the soul. Some are singing patriotic songs. Others are gathering logs to provide more permanent dwelling places. A few remain downtrodden and convinced there is no hope of winning the present battle, let alone the war.

And yet some see revival on the horizon, brought about by a new regiment of culture warriors being called to the battle line, to bear their brothers' burdens and fulfill their mission on the field of valor.

George Washington could have been speaking to us when he wrote these words to Philip Schuyler in 1777: *"We should never despair, our situation before has been unpromising and has changed for the better, so I trust, it will again. If new difficulties arise, we must only put forth new exertions and proportion our efforts to the exigency of the times."*

I heard it said once that it only took two percent of America's population back then to create our nation. And that it still would only take two percent to change it today. Like me, if you don't like what you see in America, then join me by being a part of the new two percent!

If you're with me, then I tell you plainly that the road ahead will not be easy, but the rewards (I promise you) will be ultimately glorious. As Thomas Paine challenged on December 23, 1776, in his now famous *The Crisis*, which served as a rallying call to the Continental Army, I echo as a challenge also for us:

These are the times that try men's souls. The summer soldier and the sunshine patriot will, in this crisis, shrink from the service of their country, but he that stands it now, deserves the love and thanks of man and woman. Tyranny, like hell, is not easily conquered; yet we have this consolation with us, that the harder the conflict, the more glorious the triumph.

— Chuck Norris

Save Our Sovereignty

ELEPHANTS & ASSES SCREWING THE MASSES

Drill Now In U.S.A. NOT Brazil

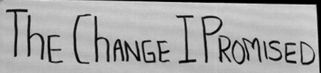

The Change I Promised

Communist in The White House
Compromising The CIA
Showing Weakness to our Enemies

Socialized Programs / Take overs

MR. SMITH CAN'T HELP US NOW

VOTE THE SOB's OUT!

I drove from Texas

To drive back

Taxe$

Principles

PULL YOUR HEAD OUT OF YOUR ASS AND YOUR HAND OUT OF MY WALLE

CHANGE WE CAN'T BELIEVE IN
READ THE CONSTITUTION

KEEP THE CHANGE

YOU LIE

"OUR MONEY"
IF YOU KEEP
SPENDING IT,
WE WILL QUIT
SENDING IT!

How GULLIBLE
AND STUPID
Do You THINK
We ARE?

HEY WASHINGTON!
IT DOESN'T
MATTER HOW
MUCH LIPSTICK
YOU PUT ON THIS
"PIG"
HR 3200
WE
DON'T
WANT
IT!

NE IF BY CAP AND TRADE!
TWO IF BY OBAMACARE!

AMERICANS WAKEUP AND
TOP THE STATISTS' AGENDA!

STOP
SOCIALIZED
MEDICINE

IT'S 9·12
..."LET'S
ROLL..."
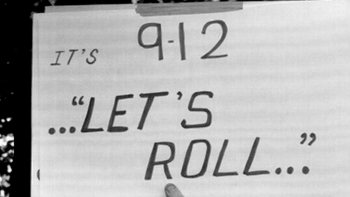

GOVERNMENT
IS THE
PROBLEM

REMEMBER,
REMEMBER the 12th
of SEPTEMBER
THE REVOLUTION
IS BREWING

COMMON   SENSE
NOT
DOLLARS & CENTS
$ ¢

IF IT SOUNDS LIKE MARX
AND ACTS LIKE STALIN
IT'S PROBABLY ☭BAMA

RESISTANCE
TO TYRANTS
IS
OBEDIENCE TO
GOD
T.J.

1984
IS NOT
AN
INSTRUCTION
MANUAL!

236 DAYS
245 SPEECHES
WHAT AN
EGO!

RATION GOVERNMENT
NOT HEALTHCARE!

AMERICANS UNITE FOR
FREEDOM FROM TYRANNY!

We Are
We the People
HEED OUR VOICE

NO
OBAMACORN
HEALTHCARE
WE NEED JOBS

Washington - "535" Liars +
37 Czars (RADICALS)
ARROGANCE
HIPOCRACY
SELF SERVING
"Tyranny by The Minority"
T. Jefferson
VOTE THE BUMS OUT & 2010
2012

· STOP THE SPENDING·
· STOP THE CORRUPTION·
· SECURE OUR BORDERS·
· NO TO GOVT·RUN HEALTHCA
"LET'S ROLL" AMERICA !!!!

ITS NOT ABOUT HEALTHCARE - ITS ABOUT CONTROL!

I'm Here Representing 9015 PLUS People

NO GOVERNMENT HEALTHCARE!

GOV'T HEALTHCARE?
CUT FRAUD NOT FREEDOM!

HANDS OFF MY HEALTH CARE!

Government Mental Healthcare
The Lunatics are guarding the Asylum!

Ted Kennedy (God Bless His Soul) Chose AMERICA For His Treatment NOT The British, France or Canada

FREEREPUBLIC.COM

AMERICA OF THE PEOPLE BY THE PEOPLE FOR THE PEOPLE
Abraham Lincoln

A
O
B
F

GOVERNMENT IS THE PROBLEM CUT THE BUDGET

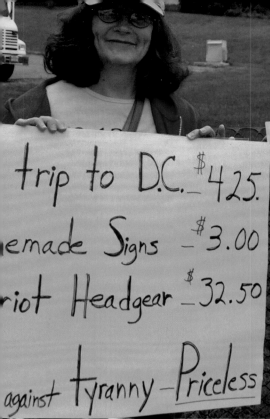

trip to D.C. - $425.
memade Signs - $3.00
riot Headgear - $32.50

against Tyranny - Priceless

You Can't F
STUPI
But you CAN VO
THEM OUT

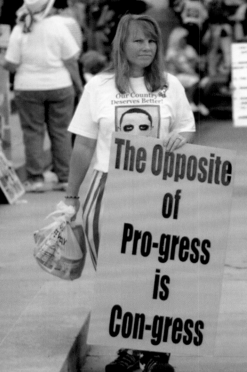

The Opposite
of
Pro-gress
is
Con-gress

We came
unarmed
(this time)

OK, JOKE'S OVER
BRING BACK THE
CONSTITUTION.
- WE ARE CITIZENS, NOT SUBJE
- REMEMBER THAT FREEDOM THING??

socialism

NOPE

socialis

socialism

NOPE

socialis

MARX WAS A MORON

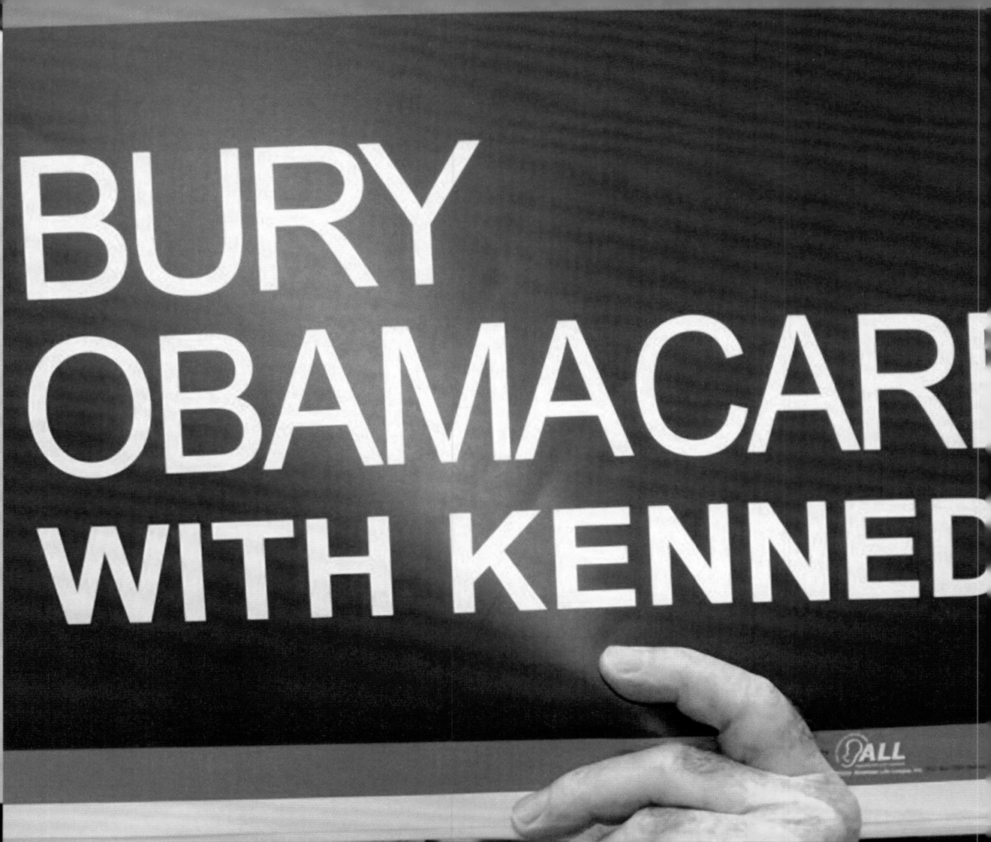

BURY OBAMACARE WITH KENNED

ALL

CAPITALISM MADE AMERICA NOT GOVERNMENT

otbell

Which One Are You Drinking?

OH, THE GOOD OLD DAYS...

REMEMBER WHEN MAO TSE-TUN
WAS A MURDERER...
NOT A MENTOR?!

MY Momma NEVER   RAISED NO MAOIST!

NO MORE

BAILOUTS!

WAKE UP &
SMELL THE
OCIALISM

U.S. ECONOMY

DID I DO THAT?

TAXED ENOUGH ALREADY!

FreeRepublic.com

BAIL-OUTS WON'T HELP UNLESS WE MAKE FREE TRADE FAIR TRADE

Liberty: All the Stimulus We Need

I'M THE OBAMA HEALTH CARE CZAR "SENIORS" SIGN YOUR BODY BAGS UP IT'S TO NOW FOR YOUR LATE BEFORE

WE ARE NOT DEMOCRATS
WE ARE NOT REPUBLICANS
WE ARE THE NEW PARTY OF COMMON SENSE

POLITICIANS LIE
PATIENTS DIE

YOU HAVE NO RIGHT TO GRAB OUR HEALTH CARE AND SCREW IT UP!

Swine Flu
Doesn't Scare Me...
Gov.'t Health Care Does!!!

On November 3 Astroturf Voted!

The SLEEPING Giant has arrived to take back it's SOVEREIGN Nation

KEN-YA TRUST OBAMA

Ron Paul

SWEEPING AWAY Socialism ONE Democrat At A TIME!!.. OH My Bad got More than one Tuesday

Senators, a vote against my Job is a vote against your Job!

STUPIDLY IS AS STUPIDLY DOES

CARBON TAX GETS U AT BOTH ENDS

WHERE'S THE BIRTH CERTIFICATE?

TAXATION WITHOUT LUBRICATION!!!

GOV. ENEMY #1

ObamaCare #'s do not Compute! Obama LIES while U.S. Treasury FRIES

Debt WILL ENSLAVE

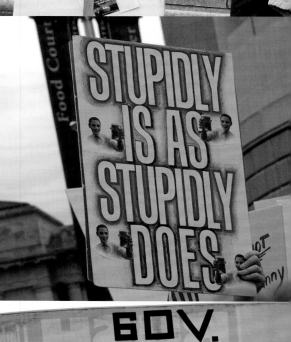

THE STATE DIDN'T GIVE US LIBERTY, GOD DID!

No More Ca$h FOR THESE
Dodd Reid Frank Waters MORAN
Hoyer Pelosi
DOUBLE TROUBLE For US. Baucus Rangel Jackson-Lee
CLUNKERS

"THOSE WHO CANNOT REMEMBER THE PAST ARE CONDEMNED TO REPEAT."
California Je

ey. Pelosi use those ~~Crazy~~ Big ~~Beautiful~~ Eyes & Look around me... ASTROTURF Does NOT Grow!

• NO TO CAP & TAX
• NO TO HEALTH CARE DISTRUCTION
• NO TO STIMULIS FUNDED MARXISTS
• NO TO DIVERSITY SENSORSHIP
• NO TO GOVERMENT TYRANNY

REGARDLESS WHERE HE WAS BORN, OBAMA IS UN - AMERICAN

WE THE PEOPLE WE THE GOVT.!

BAILOUTS + DEBT = FISCAL CHILD ABUSE

"...government of the people, by the people r the people, shall ne ish from the earth.
braham Lincoln

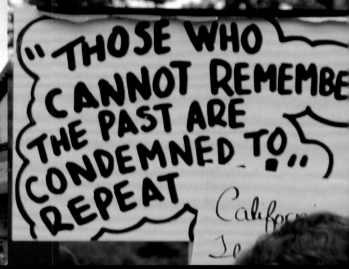

CONSERVATIVE BECAUSE SOMEONE HAS TO SUPPORT A LIBERAL

IT TOOK CARTER TO GIVE US REAGAN

Even I can't take Obamacare

YES! TORT REFORM YES! LIMIT MARX GOV'T

IF WE AIN'T BROKE DON'T FIX IT!

THERE IS NO HOPE IN SOCIALISM

Abortion IS NOT Healthcare

Nancy, The Botox tax is Going to Bankrupt Your Husband, Pau, Stop Her!

BARNEY FRANK JOHN KERRY CAN'T HEAR ME IN BOSTON... CAN YOU HEAR ME NOW? HANDS OFF MY HEALTHCARE

☑ Phone Calls
☑ E-Mail

You just won't listen, so I'm here in person...

JUST STOP   STOP

America DOES NOT WANT

Socialized Medicine

VOTE-FOR-THE BILL !!! = GET-FIRED!

You Are ELECTED TO SERVE UNDER OATH! UPHOLD THE CONSTITUTION!

ABORT OBAMA CARE NOT BABIES

IF I WANTED PORK I'D BUY A PIG

STOP SPENDING Don't Enslave Our Children

PRES. OBAMA re you listening We're Broke. TOP SPENDING

BURY OBAMACARE WITH KENNEDY

ABORTION IS NOT HEALTHCARE

ABORTION IS NOT HEALTHCARE

DON'T TAX ME BRO!

MY GRANDKIDS SAY... QUIT SPENDING OUR $$$

A JUST GOVERNMENT PROTECTS THE INDIVIDUAL'S RIGHTS TO:

LIFE
LIBERTY
PROPERTY

ANYTHING LESS IS A DERELICTION OF DUTY.
ANYTHING MORE IS AN ABUSE OF POWER.

The Constitution

We the People.....

FREEDOM

It's not just a good ide

It's the LAW

IF FREEDOM IS WHAT WE WANT IT IS OURS FOR THE TAKING
- RON PAUL

I AM THE PeoPLE YOURE FiReD!

Liar Liar Pants on fire!

We the People

(REMEMBER US)

OBAMACARE IS to health care as the vaccine is to Swineflu
The 'CURE' IS WORSE than the 'ILLNESS'

You Can't Fix Stupid but You can "Vote it Out!"

A CLEAN SWEEP IN 2010!

Pelosi

Boeclerl   Ryan

LIAR LIAR COUNTRY ON FIRE

AMERICA WE DON'T REDISTRIBUTE WE EARN IT! SPREAD MY WORK ETHIC NOT MY WEALTH

INVESTIGATE OBAMA AND HIS CZARS NOT THE CIA

FROM DEMOCRACY TO SOCIALISM TO FACISM IN EIGHT MONTHS

STOP OBAMA'S DEATH PANELS

Fiscal Irresponsibility Is The Change I canNot believe in!

10% = Enough for GOD ~
10% = Enough for the IRS

BEND OVER

HERE COMES CHANGE

"HOW CAN I BLES
THIS NATION
WHEN THE BLOOD
OF THE BABIES
CRIES TO ME
FROM THE GROUND"

R_CYCLE
CONGRESS
SAVE
AMERICA !

On second thought...
Don't read the bill.
READ THE
CONSTITUTION !!

THE TEA PARTY
Florida   Florida
We're Watching
every vote you cast

CHANGE
YES
HOPE
???

MR. PRESIDENT
WHERE'S THE
BIRTH CERTIFICATE!

MEDICARE IS BROKE
MEDICAID IS BROKE
SOCIAL SECURITY IS BROKE
Our Country
Is Bankrupt

MD
NOT
ATM

STOP
BANKRUPTING
MY
COUNTRY

~Obama~
LIE
after
LIE
after
LIE
~   ~

BAD LAWS ARE
– THE WORST –
SORT OF TRYANNY

~Edmund Burke

We Were WRONG!
Clinton Had A Better
"STIMULUS"
Plan

"Dependence begets subservience and venality, suffocates the germ of virtue, and prepares fit tools for the designs of ambition."

TYRANNY

Comes in a
Smiley Face!

★ Don't Punish
the 85% 4 the
15% that don't
Have Insurance

YOU
WORK
for US!
We the People

"Fundamentally Change America"
Obama
Over My Dead Body

X-COUCH
POTATO
WHO is BOILED

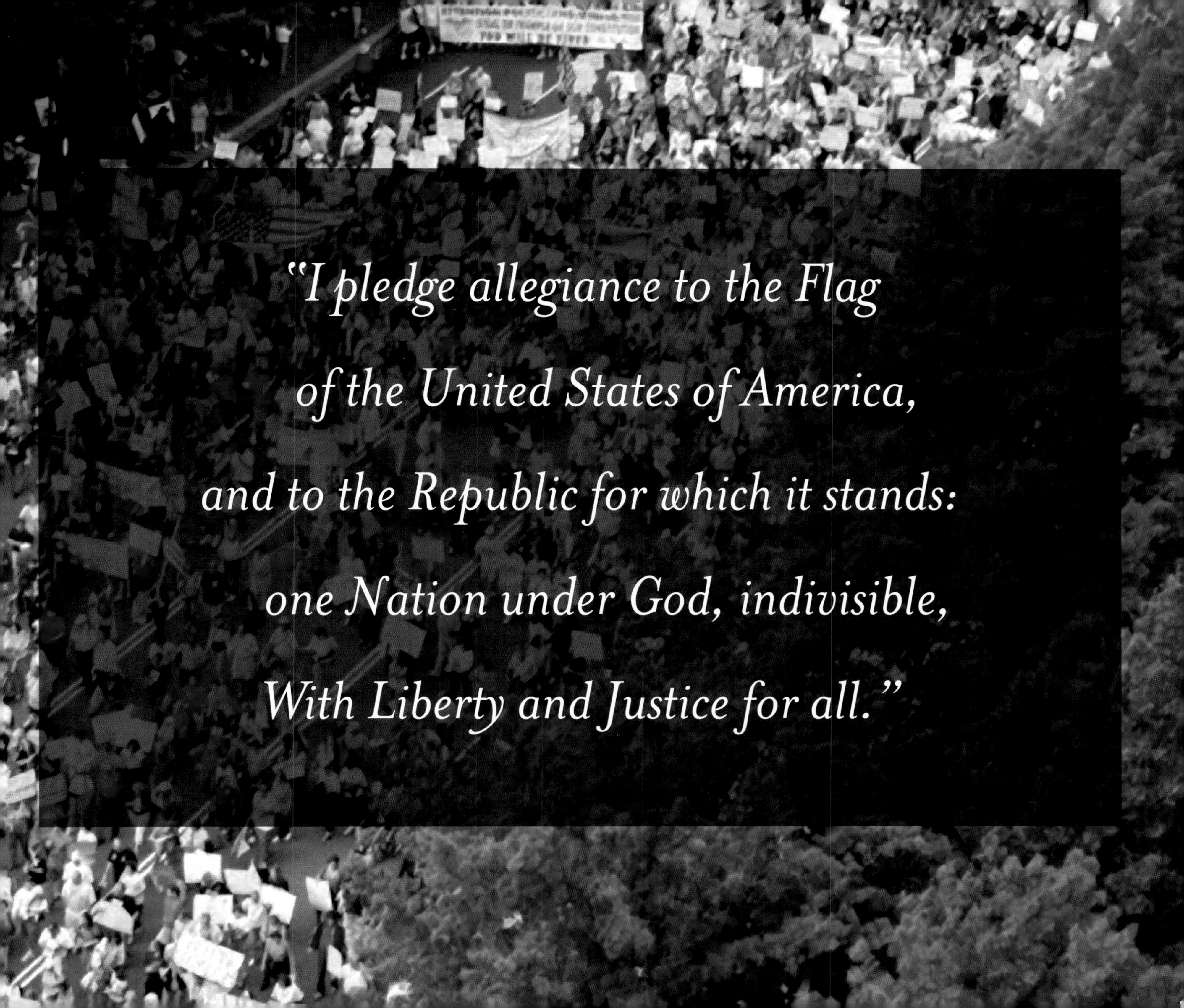

"I pledge allegiance to the Flag

of the United States of America,

and to the Republic for which it stands:

one Nation under God, indivisible,

With Liberty and Justice for all."

Who's HAD

IF I WANTED TO BE COMM- MUNIST I WOULD MOVE TO RUSSIA

Ali bama & the 40 Czar where's the CHECK & BALANC

LIARS and COMMIES and CZARS OH MY!

THE ORIGIN OF THE S

SAVE GRANNY DEFEAT OBAMACARE

1 CZAR DOWN 43 to Go Congress? 2010

CONSTITUTION ???
GOTCHA SUCKERS !!!

RANSPARENT?
I SEE THRU
YOUR LIES
SOCIALIST
FOOL

"HEY CAPITOL HILL"
IN 2011
YOU'RE ALL FIRED !
YOU JUST DON'T
KNOW IT YET !

WE WANT THE
SAME
HEALTHCARE
AS
TED KENNEDY
AND
CONGRESS

BarACK
OFF

CASH FOR CLUNKERS TRADE IN YOUR CONGRESSMAN

OBAMA'S CHURC

BLACK SUPREMACIST

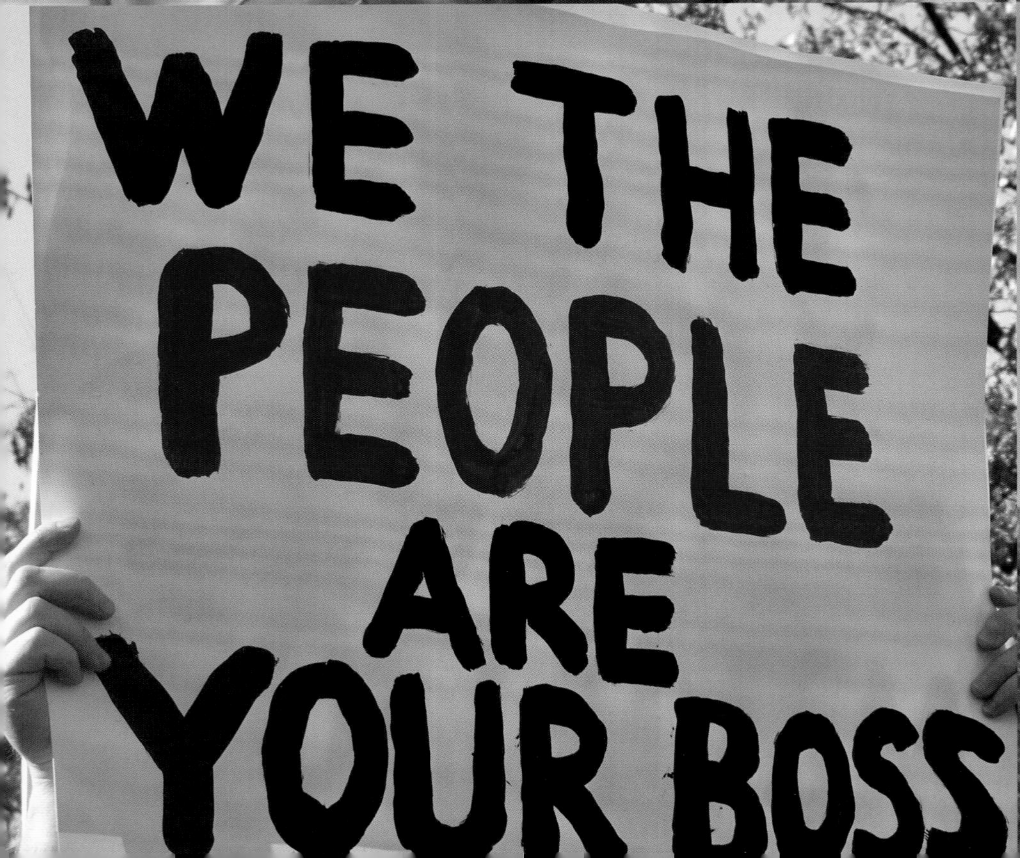

WE THE PEOPLE ARE YOUR BOSS

"GIVING MONEY & POWER TO THE GOVERNMENT IS LIKE GIVING WHISKEY & CAR KEYS TO TEEN-AGE BOYS"

P.J. O'ROURKE

Where's
The
Birth
Certificate
?

HIGH TAXES
+ BIG GOVERNME
= SLAVERY

ANOTHER
SMALL
BUSINESS
CASUALTY

HOUSTON SAY
No To Pork
EXCEPT AT
RODEO

HEAR U.S.
T.E.A.
TAXED
ENOUGH
ALREADY!
NOW
OR VOTED
OUT LATER

LIVE ON A
UDGET SO
HOULD
OVERNMENT

SAVE MY POT
OF GOLD
NO MORE BAILOUTS

PROTECT
OUR
FREEDOM
OF
SPEECH

I'M JUST 7 YRS
OLD
I'M A FINANCIA
WIZARD AND
KNOW I'M BRO

March on D.C.
9.12.09
Tennessee

Nancy Kiss my ...STROTURF

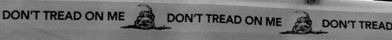

DON'T TREAD ON ME   DON'T TREAD ON ME   DON'T TREAD ON ME

"I predict future happiness for Americans if they can prevent the government from wasting the labors of the people under the pretense of taking care of them."

THOMAS JEFFERSON.

THE DEMOCRAT PARTY WELCOMES YOU TO THE USSA

SAVE GRANDMA PULL THE PLU ON CONGRESS

WAKE UP
AMERICA
STOP THE
INSANITY

BACK OFF!

DONT TREAD ON ME

WE'RE NOT
WEE-WEED UP
WE'RE
PISSED OFF!

GIVE US
BACK OUR
COUNTRY!!
We the People

OBAMMUNISM
IS
COMMUNISM

OBAMA
SUCKS

IT'S TIME
TO DRAIN
THE SWAMP
IN D.C.

YOU LIES!

If you vote for this Health Care
I WILL SUPPORT
YOUR OPPONE

BAMACARE

NO BIG BRO

OCIALISM

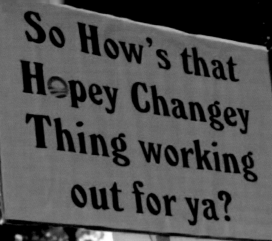

So How's that Hopey Changey Thing working out for ya?

THERE'S FREE CHEESE in a MOUSETRAP

REAGANITE

Real Nurses CYBER CAD CONTROL TAX TARP NO-BAMA-CARE BAILOUTS CZARS

OBAMA IS ACORN

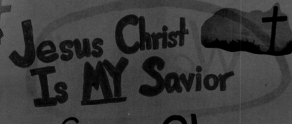

Jesus Christ Is MY Savior

So Sorry Obama Is Yours

Obamacare makes me SICK

HEY CONGRESS *IT'S ME AGAIN.* LET'S TAKE THE CROSSHAIRS OFF THE JOB CREATORS!

SMALL BUSINESS

KALAMAZOO, MICHIGAN

OBAMA'S NUTS!

ACORN

FREEDOM

BEND OVER

TOXIC ASSETS:
- ☒ Van Jones
- ☐ Cass Sunstein
- ☐ John Holdren
- ☐ Mark Lloyd
- ☐ Carol Browner

End the Infestation!

I WANT YOU
TO FOOT THE BILL

Since 1630
Bible hugging!
Gun toting!
Red Blooded
    American!
Against
Tyranny

VAN JONES GONE

ONE DOWN

33 TO GO!

OBAMA

SIZE MATTERS
REDUCE GOVERNMENT

LET NO GOVERNMENT
EXIST
THAT IS NOT
RESPONSIBLE
TO THE PEOPLE

Californians Against Obamacare

"*I would much prefer to bring them down as soon as possible. I think they've made the biggest financial mess that any government's ever made in this country for a very long time, and the Socialist governments traditionally do make a financial mess. They always run out of other people's money. It's quite characteristic of them. They then start to nationalize everything, and people just do not like more and more nationalization, and they're now trying to control everything by other means. They're progressively reducing the choice available to ordinary people.*"

(Margaret Thatcher during an interview on February 5, 1976)

"The problem with Socialism is that eventually you run out of other people's money"
Margaret Thatcher

SELL YOUR BOAT & PAY FOR YOUR OWN HEALTH CARE

POLITICANS WHERE ARE THE JOBS LISTEN TO OUR VOICES

STOP THE CONGRESS RUINING AMERICA'S PROSPERITY

IN GOD WE TRUST PRAY FOR OU LIBERTY !

TRANSPARENCY
OBAMA STYLE
CARD CHECK

SECRET BALLOTS
FAGETTA BOUT IT

MR PRESIDENT
A HALFTRUT
IS OFTEN A
BIG LIE !

If You Are Not
Outraged, You
Must Not Pay Taxes

OBAMA
WE <u>ARE</u> A JUDEO
CHRISTIAN NATION
GOD HAS BLESSED US
BY HONORING HIM

$ HOLD THEM
ACCOUNTABLE
FOR THEIR LIES
—
TERM LIMITS!
—
WE THE PEOPLE

AGAINST
ALL
ENEMIES
FOREIGN
<u>AND</u>
DOMESTIC

OFFICIAL PACE CAR

OFFICIAL PACE CAR

OBAMACAR

TEA PARTY
TODAY
TAR AND FEATHERS
TOMORROW

WE ARE
NOT "Astroturf"
NOT "A Mob"
NOT "Nazis"
WE ARE
FED UP!

Obama ...
the Enemy
of
LIBERTY

CONFISCATION OF WAGES IS SLAVERY

OOD COP BAD COU

SAME TEAM WITH A SCHEME

Get the ACORN OUT OF YOUR EARS AND LISTEN TO USA

FIX THE ECONOMY

HEY... I got the WRONG CHANGE!

STOP
SPENDING
YOU'RE
STEALING
TAXPAYERS'
MONEY!

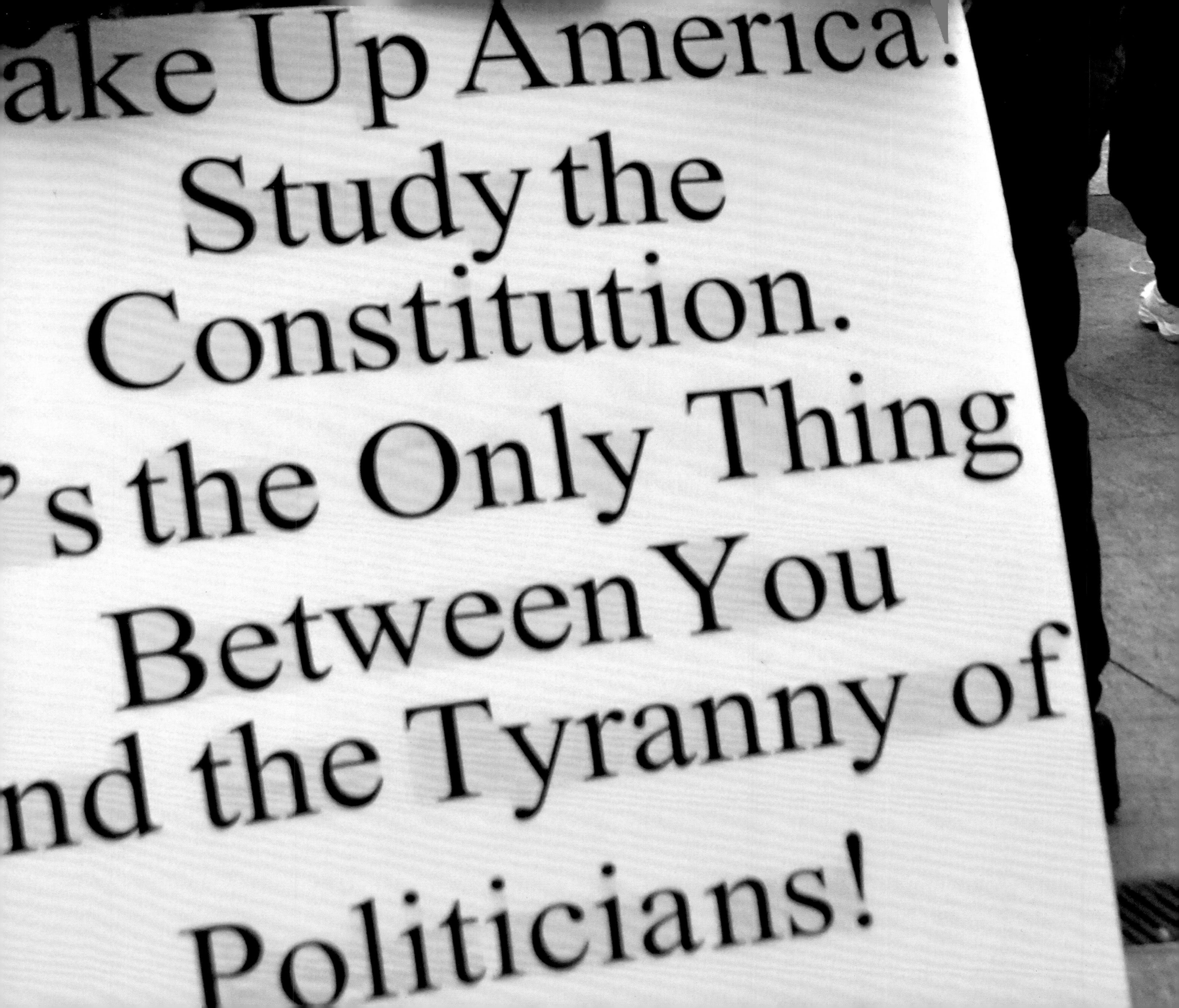

ake Up America!
Study the
Constitution.

's the Only Thing
Between You
nd the Tyranny of
Politicians!

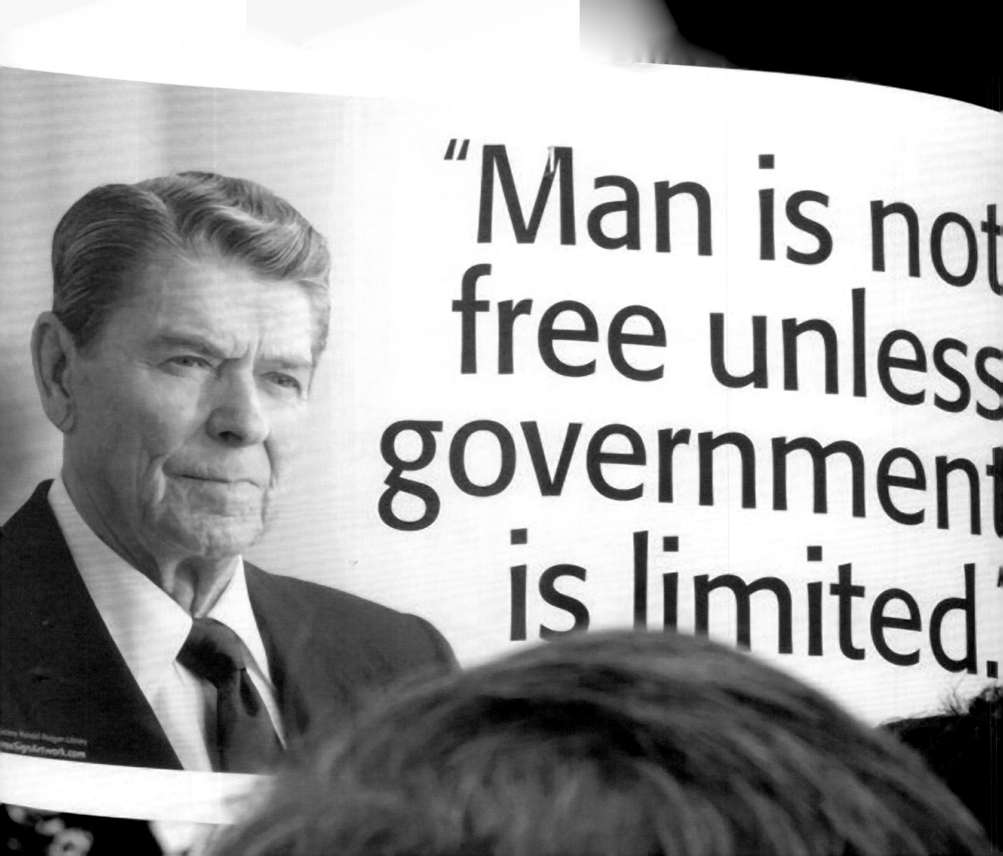

"It is time for us to realize that we're too great a nation to limit ourselves to small dreams. We're not, as some would have us believe, doomed to an inevitable decline. I do not believe in a fate that will fall on us no matter what we do. I do believe in a fate that will fall on us if we do nothing. So, with all the creative energy at our command, let us begin an era of national renewal. Let us renew our determination, our courage, and our strength. And let us renew our faith and our hope. We have every right to dream heroic dreams. Those who say that we're in a time when there are no heroes, they just don't know where to look."

(Ronald Reagan — from his first inaugural address 1981)

NOBAMA CARE

Think Government Health Care Won't **Think Again.**

Government-Run Health Care. Sticking it to the Taxpayers.

NOVEMBER 3, 2009 WAS JUDGEMENT DAY IN VIRGINIA & NEW JERSEY

NOVEMBER 2, 2010 WILL BE JUDGEMENT DAY FOR THE US CONRESS.

WE DON'T THINK YOU HEARD US ON — 9-12-09 — WE HOPE YOU CAN — READ! — NO HEALTH CARE WHAT PART OF FREEDOM DON'T YOU UNDER STAND

NO OBAMA CARE

Stop Spending my Kids Future!

OBAMA MADOFF WITH CAPITALISM & THE CONSTITUTION

BEST FRIENDS

socialism

OBAMA CARE GRAVE-YARD SHOVEL-READY FOR SENIORS

No More ¢A$H For These CLUNKERS!

THE PARTY IS OVER.

Swine Flu genocide DO NOT take the vaccine!

MAN IS NOT FREE UNLESS GOVERNMENT IS LIMITED

CONGRESS PINK SLIP

STOP REWARDING FAILURE · LET FAILURES FAIL · STOP PUNISHING SUCCESS

GOVERNMENT IS THE PROBLEM NOT THE SOLUTION

STAND AGAINST BO IT SMELLS BAD

JOE WILSON WAS RIGHT! YOU LIE APOLOGIZE TO AMERICA!

CONGRESS YOUR VOTE IS ON THE INTERNET

READ THE U.S. CONSTITUION

I ONCE WAS BLIND AND NOW I SEE

CHANGE IS ALL WE'LL HAVE LEFT!

He's Right U Lie !!

YOU CAN'T DEBATE WITH LIARS

COMMUNIST HAVE A NEW GENERATION EXECUTIONER

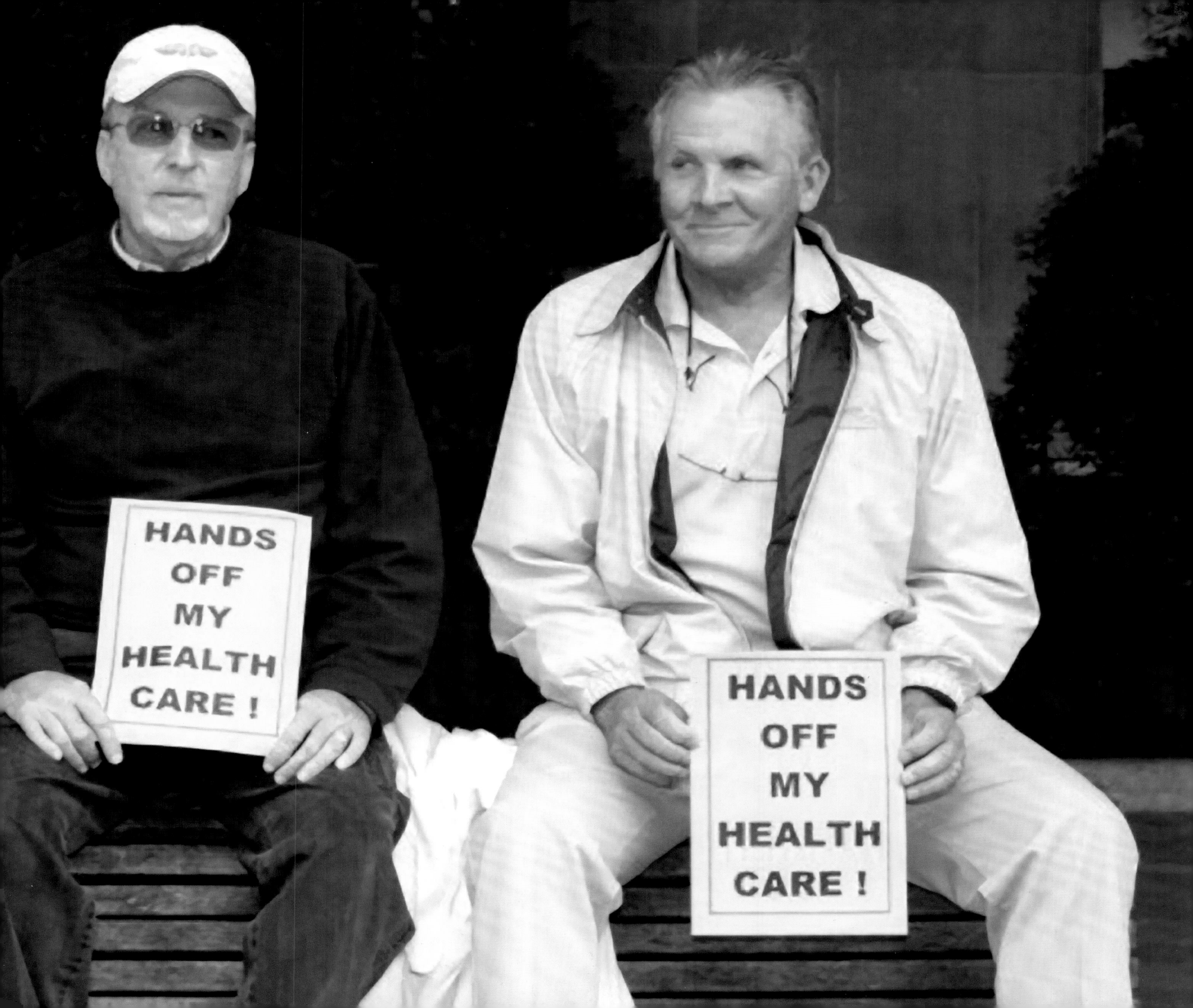
HANDS
OFF
MY
HEALTH
CARE !
HANDS
OFF
MY
HEALTH
CARE !

GHT LIBERAL FASCISM!

TOP OBAMA!

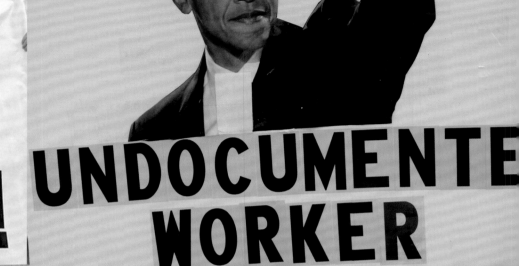

UNDOCUMENTE WORKER

MOST POLITICIAN ARE ORGANIZED CRIMINALS

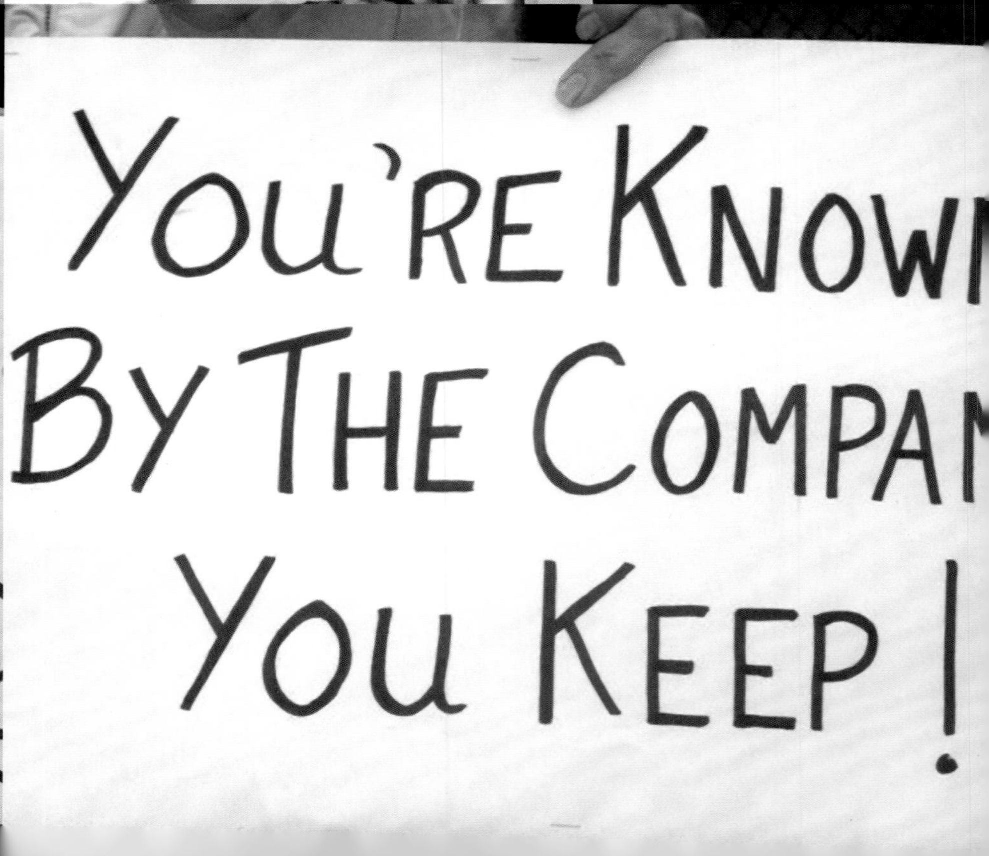

YOU'RE KNOWI BY THE COMPAN YOU KEEP!

BEND OVER AMERICA

Oh! The Lies

If it's not good enough for CONGRESS it's not good enough for ME!

THE PERPETRATORS OF THE GLOBAL WARMING HOAX, WANT TO CONTROL OUR LIVES & STEAL OUR MONEY

If I Handled my money like the GOVERNMENT I'd be in PRISON!

THIS IS ALL THE CHANGE I HAVE!

Enterprise

LEARN CHINESE YOU WILL NEED IT!!

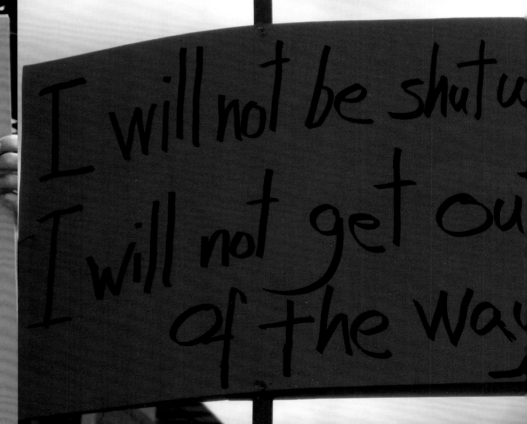

I will not be shut u

I will not get ou

of the way

Social Security
Medicare — Broke
Medicaid — Broke
Amtrak — Broke
Post Office — Broke
Freddie & Fannie — Broke
But the Feds think
They can run Healthcare?
THINK AGAIN!

PELOSI NEEDS A NOSE JOB

WE ♥ CIA

OBAMA
Cuban Americans
can recognize
Socialist agenda

OUR LAWMAKERS
ARE SMOKING
DISCOUNT
DOPE!!

GOVERNMENT
IS THE
PROBLEM

YOU GIVE
TERRORISTS
FREEDOM — WHY
TAKE AWAY
OURS?
SAVE GITMO!

IT DOESN'T
MATTER WHAT
THIS SIGN SAYS
YOU'LL CALL
IT RACIST
ANYWAY

CAPITALISM
WORKS
ASK ANY
ILLEGAL ALIEN

SO HOW'S
THAT STIMULUS

THE OBAMA
WRECKOVERY
WORKING FOR
YOU??

SOCIALISM IS AN
AGGRESSIVE CANCER.
IT IS CURED ONLY
BY EARLY DETECTION.

STOP SPENDING MY MONEY!

HAVEN'T EVEN EARNED IT YET!!

TRANSPARENT? I SEE THRU YOUR LIES SOCIALIST FOOL

GOVT SPENDING IS DOO DOO ECONOMICS

SOMEWHERE IN KENYA A VILLAGE IS MISSING AN IDIOT!

10% FAIR LAWS AND TAXES

THE BEST TAX ADVISORS I'VE EVER HAD (EXCEPT FOR ACORN)

PAY ATTENTION OBAMA THIS IS A TEACHABLE MOMENT

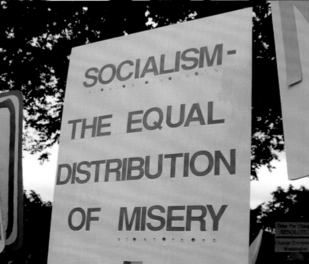

SOCIALISM- THE EQUAL DISTRIBUTION OF MISERY

OBAMACARE

TAXED ENOUGH ALREADY

THE REAL TERRORIST'S ARE IN D.C.

1·20·13
Obama's Last Day.

FRIEDMAN NOT MARX

MARK OF THE BEAST?

Vote the Bums Out!!

OUR LAWMAKERS ARE SMOKING DISCOUNT DOPE!!

I HOPE MY CHILDREN DON'T HAVE 2 WEAR THIS HAT

Remember 9/11

"*The powers not delegated to the United States by the Constitution, nor prohibited by it to the States, are reserved to the States respectively, or to the people.*"

(*The Bill of Rights — United States Constitution*)

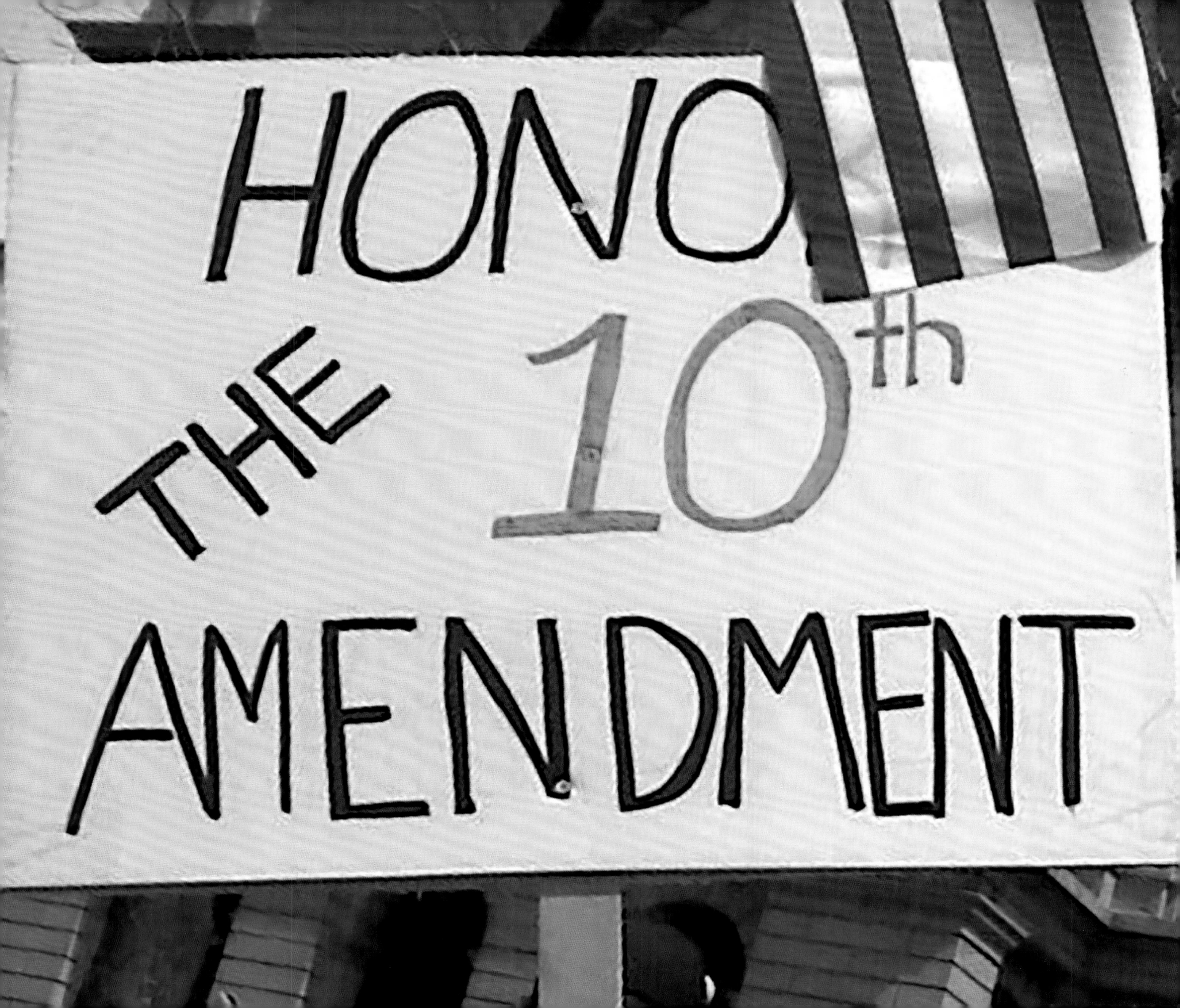
HONO
THE 10th
AMENDMENT

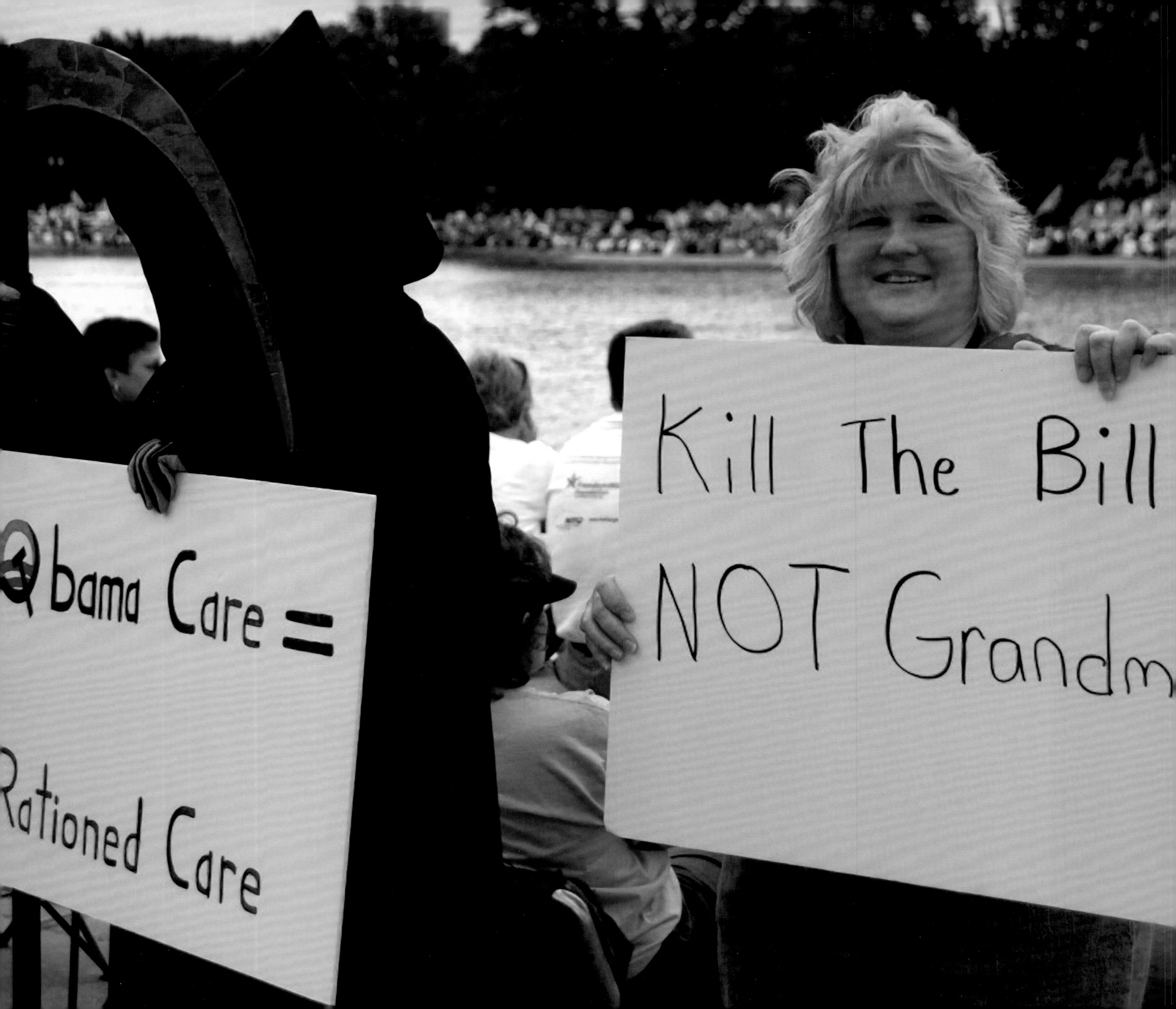
Obama Care =
Rationed Care
Kill The Bill
NOT Grandm

WAKE UP AMERICA

II Chronicles 7:14

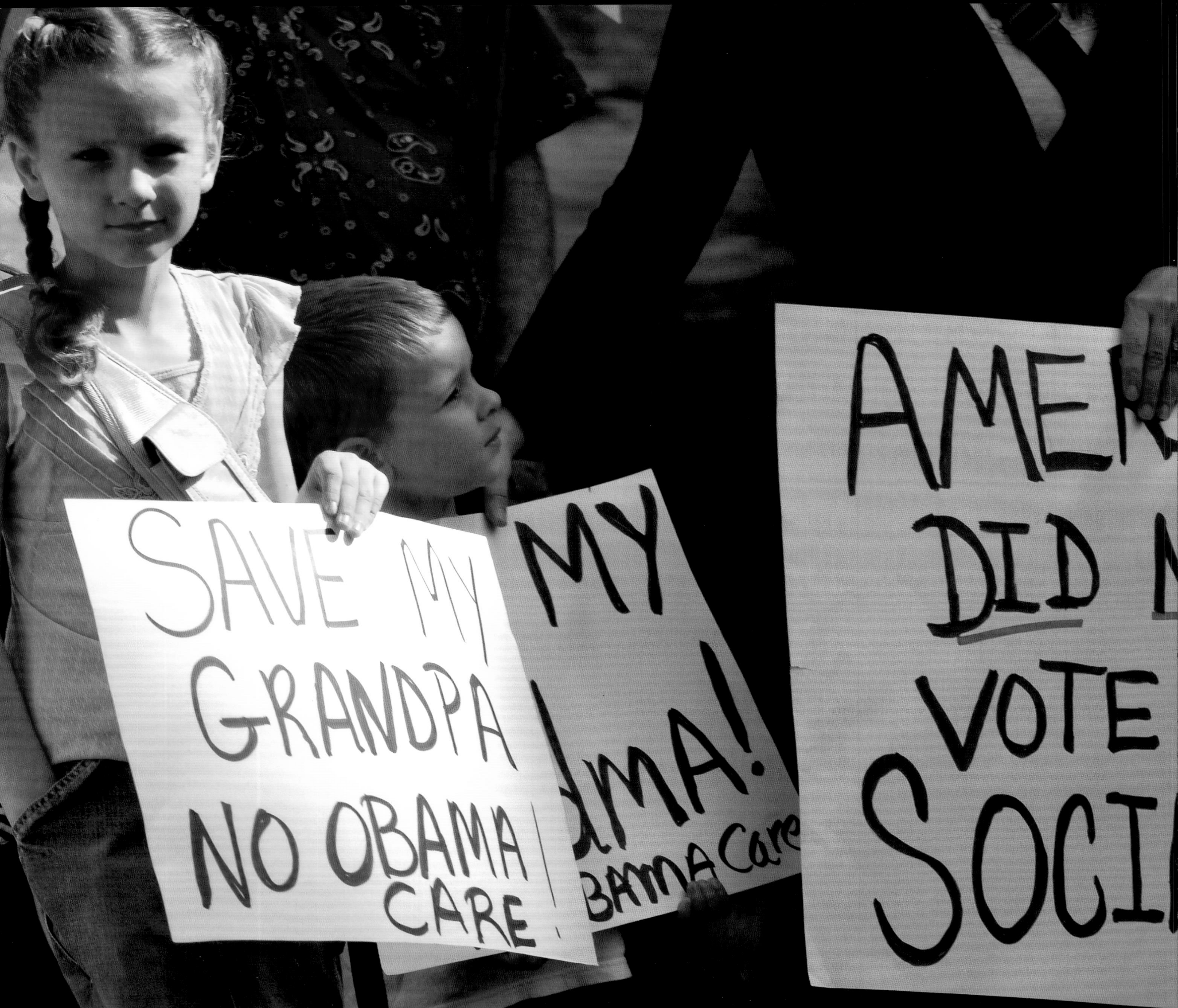
SAVE MY GRANDPA
NO OBAMA CARE!
MY
DID
VOTE

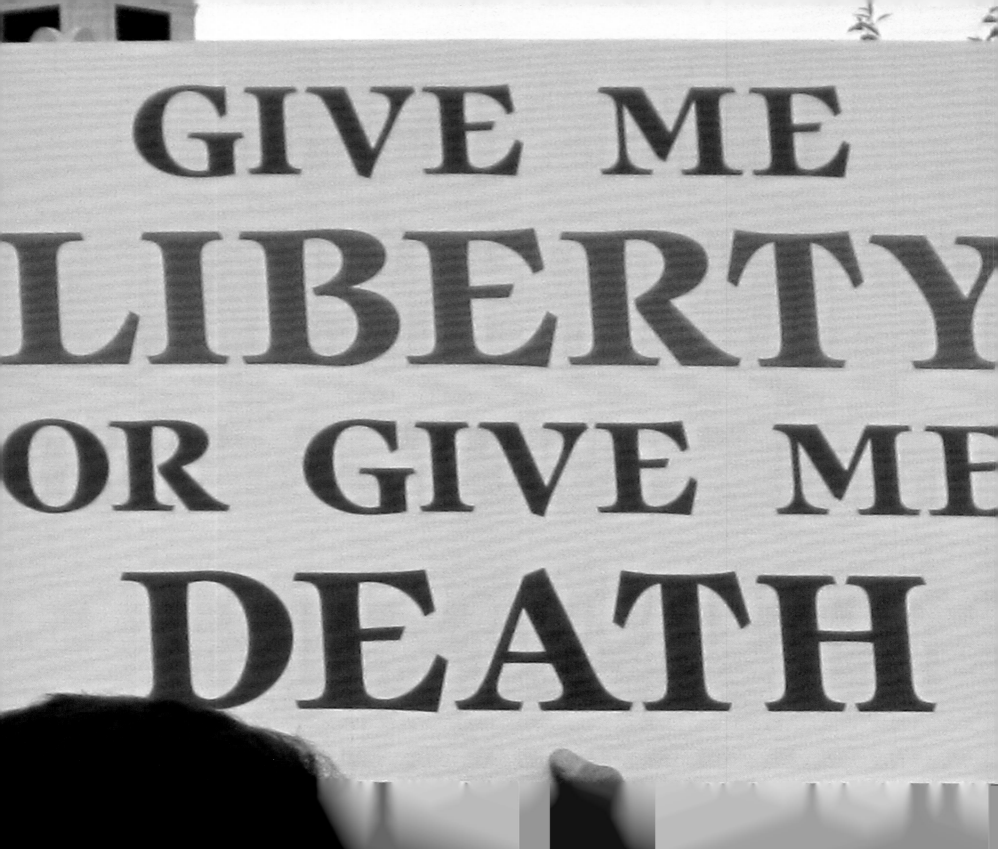

"It is in vain, sir, to extenuate the matter. Gentlemen may cry, Peace, Peace — but there is no peace. The war is actually begun! The next gale that sweeps from the north will bring to our ears the clash of resounding arms! Our brethren are already in the field! Why stand we here idle? What is it that gentlemen wish? What would they have? Is life so dear, or peace so sweet, as to be purchased at the price of chains and slavery? Forbid it, Almighty God! I know not what course others may take; but as for me, give me liberty or give me death!"

(Patrick Henry — from a speech made before the House of Burgesses in 1775)

VETERANS FOR A STRONG AMERICA

CAN YOU Hear US NOW?

Hey OBAMA WAKE UP AND SMI

STOP MAKING PRO
ThePeoples

REPORT ALL CAPITALIST ACTIVI
TO FLAG@WHITEHOUSE.GOV

$

ANGRY
AND I VOTE!

YOUR WALLET....
THE ONLY PLACE
DEMOCRATS
ARE WILLING
TO DRILL!

IOWA

DON'T SHARE
MY WEALTH,
SHARE MY
WORK ETHIC!

Born Fr
Taxed
Death

esus
MY BOSS

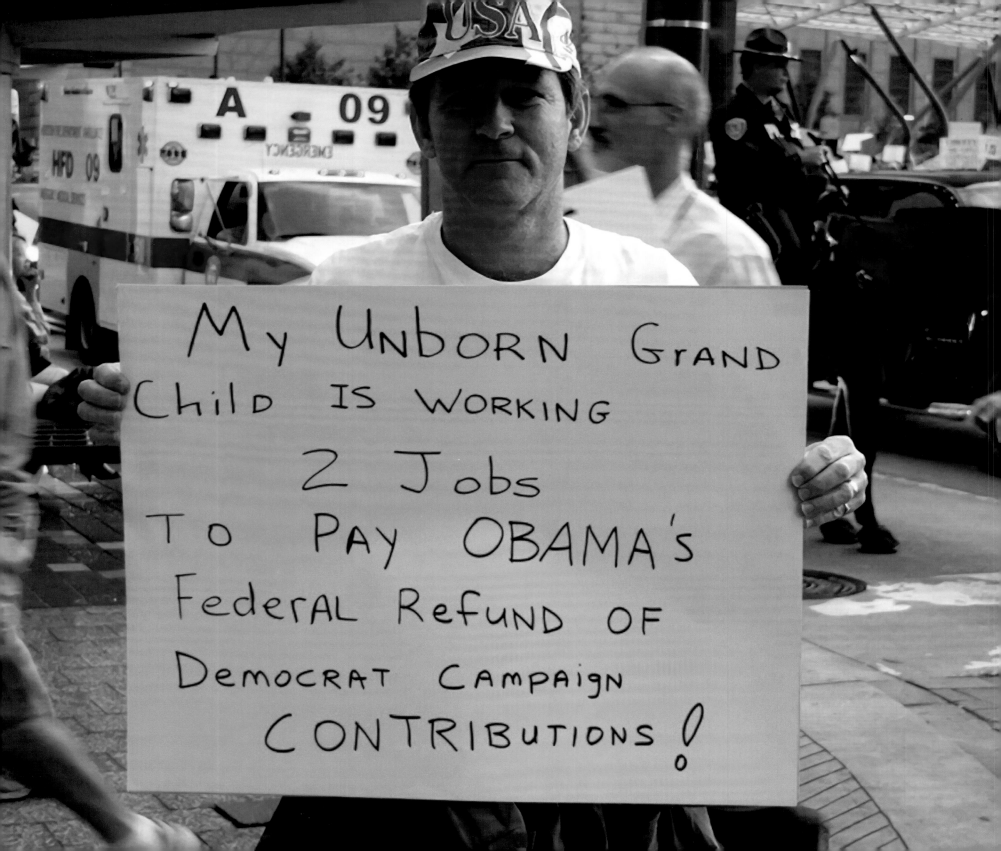

Standing for Life, Liberty + Capitalism

Mr. Obama: Where are you and **Ms. Pelosi** taking U.S.? And why are we in this HAND BASKET??

IF OBAMA'S BIRTH CERTIFICATE IS LEGAL, WHY IS HE SPENDING $1,000,000 TO CONCEAL IT?

Founding Fathers of Socialist Health Care

WE CAN HELP
THE POOR
WITHOUT GOV.
HEALTH CARE
CLIENT

Pelosi, Reid
And Obama
3 Stooges
and 2 Boob
eform Congress.o

USS IWO JIMA
LPH-2

CZAR STRANGLED
BANNER

SAVE
OUR
COUNTRY
FROM
CONGRESS

Tri
and
no
a
Ch

CZARS
BELON
IN RUSS
THROW
THEM
OUT

END

THE MEANS JUSTIFY THE

CHANGE   HOPE

WELCOME BACK, CARTER

NO MARX
NO MAO

Don't Tax Me, Bro!

QUIT WASTING OUR MONEY

STOP SPENDING START CUTTING

"CHANGE

HITLER GAVE GREAT SPEECHES TOO!

U WORK FOR US! IM HERE TO TAKE BACK AMERICA

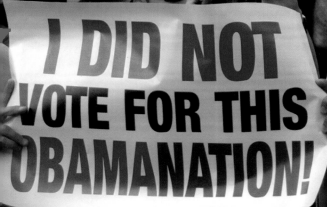

I DID NOT VOTE FOR THIS OBAMANATION!

10 YEAR $9,000,000,000,000 DEFICIT !!! RIDICULOUS STOP IT NOW

SPINNING IN THEIR GRAVES

GIVE ME LIBERTY OR GIVE ME DEATH

KILL THE BILL

OBAMMUNISM IS COMMUNISM

IS THE CONSTITUTION ANOTHER THING YOU HAVEN'T READ?

IAM NOT A SOCIALIST NO GOVERN- MENT HEALTH CARE

1900 PAGES !?! OUT WITH QUEEN BEE PELOSI

CLEAN The HOUSE 2010

FREE- DOM NOW!

OBAMA LIES!

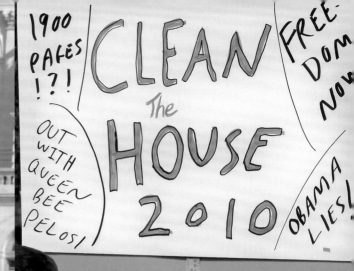

TYRANNY RESPONSE TEAM

OBAMA AND HIS MARXIST BUDDIES ARE AFTER YOUR FREEDOM

CAP & TRADE

SOCIALIZED HEALTHCARE KILLS

UBLIC HEALTH CARE A TRAGIC COMEDY

STARRING OUR GOVERNMENT

UPHOLD THE CONSTITUTION DOWN WITH TYRANNY

THANK A VET!

SILENT NO MORE!

SILENT NO MORE!

I'm A "BITTER" Gun Owner, & I VOTE

RIFLE

JOE WILSON FOR RESIDENT

END THE FED

OBEY THE CONSTITUTION

NEVER FORGET... WE ARE THE PEOPLE SPEAK W/O FEAR

I THOUGHT HE SAID CHANGE, NOT CHAIN$!

WHEN THEY CAME AFTER
• CHRISTIANS & JEWS
• REPUBLICANS
• "WE THE PEOPLE"
CONGRESS SAID NOTHING!!
WHEN THEY GO AFTER CONGRESS — WHO WILL??

STOP SPENDING OUR GRANDCHILDREN FUTURE SPEND TODAY PAY TODAY

Silent Fool NO MORE!

...NO MORE!!!

WE WILL VOTE YOU OUT

CLUELESS

OUT OF TOUCH (WITH

WHEN OBAMA LIES FREEDOM DIES

I RESIST THE UNAUTHORIZED GOVERNMENT TAKEOVER OF MY LIBERTY AND MY MONEY!

TAX PAYERS MARCH SEPTEMBER 12, 2009

COME 2012, You're leaving town!

STOP FUNDING ACORN!

I AM NOT YOUR ATM

SOMETHING STINKS IN D.C.

IT'S B.O.

IS THIS YOUR PRESIDENT?

How Many Lies Does Obama Have to Tell Before You Realize He's a Liar!

MONEY DOESN'T GROW ON TREES

SOME OF US WORK FOR IT!

Soc. Sec. : Broke
Medicare : Broke
Medicaid : Broke
ObamaCare : Priceless!

IQ Test

ou inherit the worst economy since the Depression . You:

	Score:
A. Cut spending	140
B. Increase savings	138
C. Cut taxes	125
D. Balance budget	101
F. Socialize medicine	49

IQ Test

What is the most endangered species?

A. Snail Darter
B. Spotted Owl
C. Whooping Crane
D. Kangaroo Rat
E. Congressmen who vote to socialize medicin

Play by the rules
Read the
Constitution
You Work For US

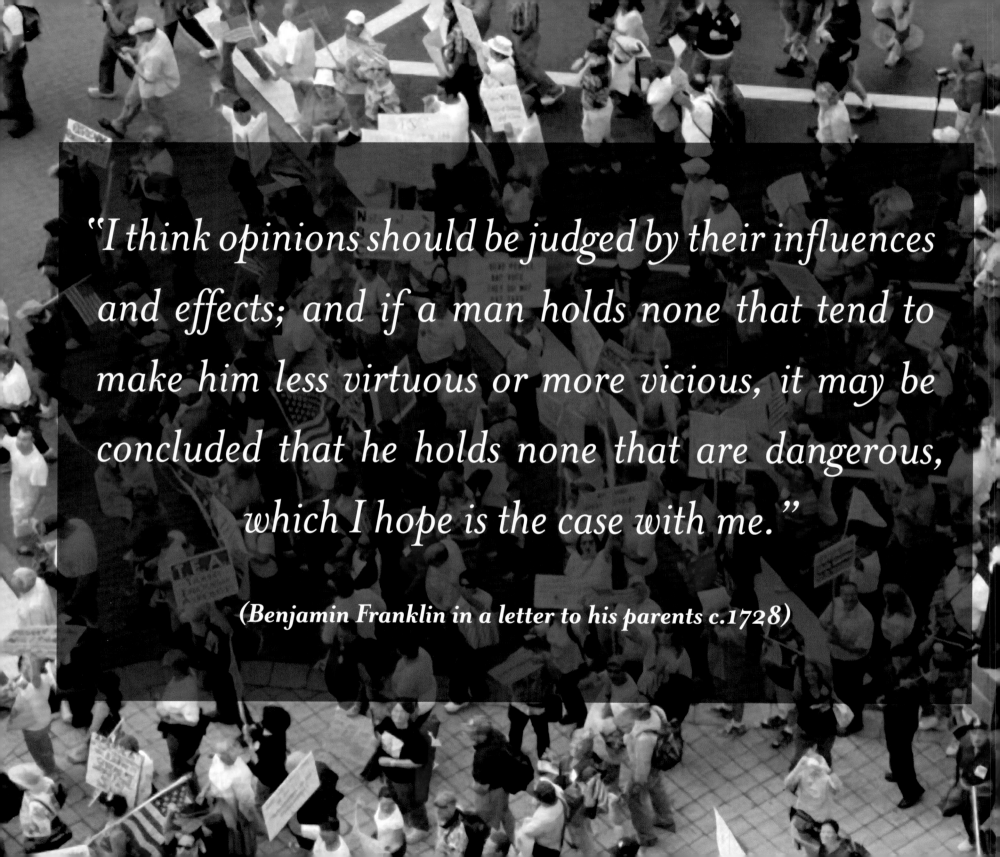

"I think opinions should be judged by their influences and effects; and if a man holds none that tend to make him less virtuous or more vicious, it may be concluded that he holds none that are dangerous, which I hope is the case with me."

(Benjamin Franklin in a letter to his parents c.1728)

"He that lives on hope will die fasting."

Benjamin Franklin 1758

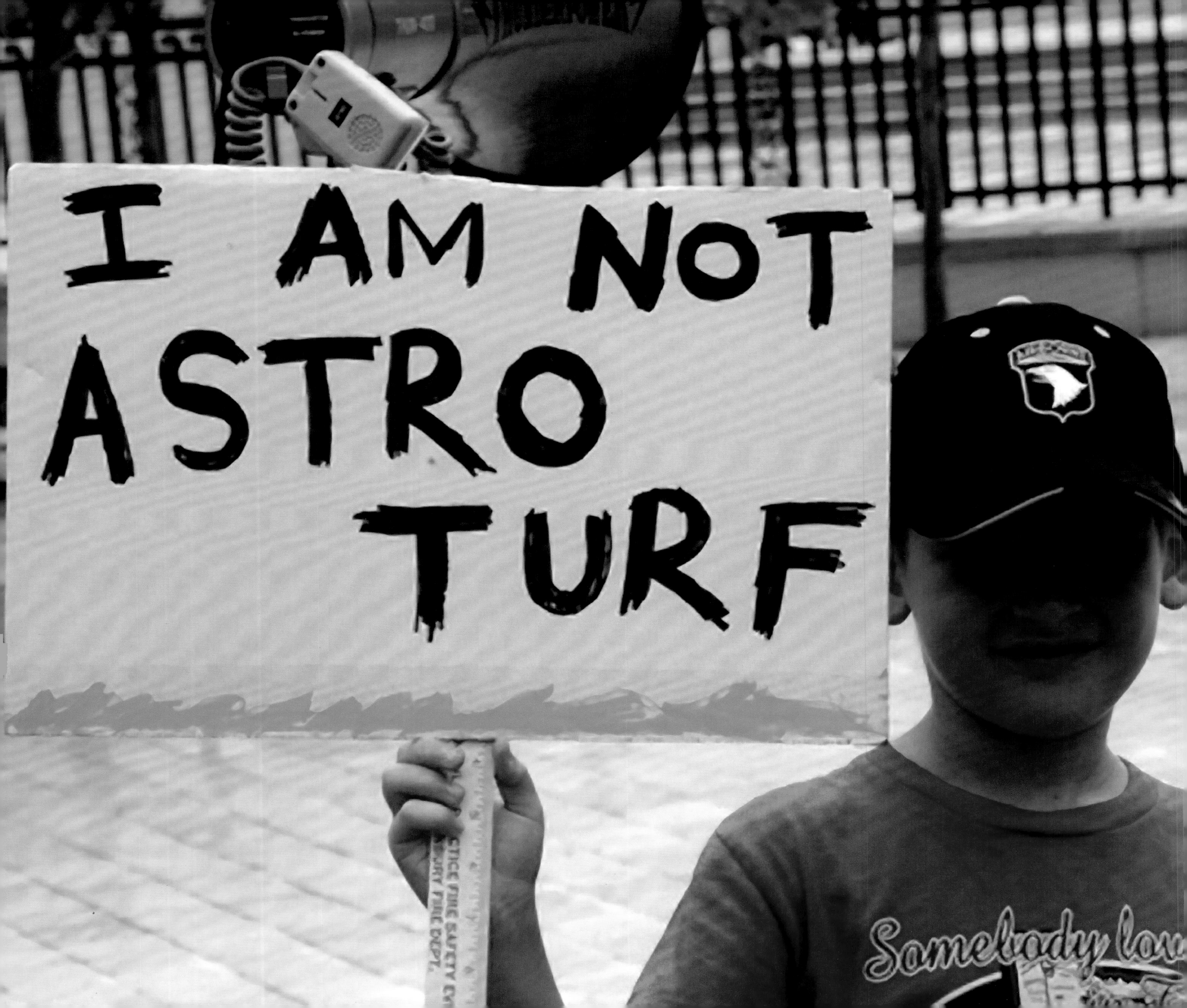
I AM NOT
ASTRO
TURF

The Second Amendment

VOID WHERE PROHIBITED BY LAW?

SAY NO TO B.O.

OBAMA LIE: ÷ CAPITALISM DIE

Stand Up To Government They Work For US!

Spread Manure Not My MONEY!

A PICTURE THIS TIME

DON'T MAKE ME COME BACK!

EVICT AND DEPORT

SOCIALIS

REPORT ALL DISSENT

YOU CAN BE REPLACED 2010

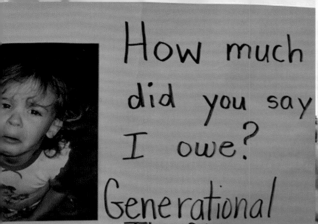

How much did you say I owe? Generational Theft

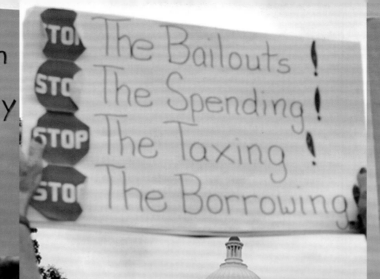

STOP STOP STOP STOP The Bailouts! The Spending! The Taxing! The Borrowing

STOP GOV'T TAKEOVER

CULTURE OF CORRUPTION

ACORN CRUSHER   TIME TO THESE BUST UP NUTS!

IMPEACH COMRADE OBAMA

If You Can't Read It How Can You Pass It?

SOCIALIZED MEDICINE HOTLINE 1800-YOUDEAD

MOVE TO CANADA

☐—TEABAG

NANCY
PELOSI

NEVER IN U.S. history
HAVE SO FEW
TAKEN SO MUCH
AND DID SO LiTTLE
COST SO MUCH

I'LL KEEP MY
GUNS, FREEDOM,
& MONEY
YOU KEEP
THE CHANGE

THOMAS   JEFFERSO
NOT
KARL   MARX
(STAY FOCUSED, DEMOCRATS
AND REPUBLICANS)

DENVER ANTI TAX
TEA PARTY

OMALI PIRATES ATTACK OUR
US SHIPS! THEY'RE
MUSLIM!

UR MUSLIM IN THE WHITE HOU
TTACKS SHIP OF STATE!

VETERAN
BLE GOV'T!

SHAKEN
AND
STIRRED

FREEDOM SLAVE

GIVE ME
LIBERTY
NOT DEBT!

RIGHT WING RADICALS

AYN RAND

WAS

RIGHT

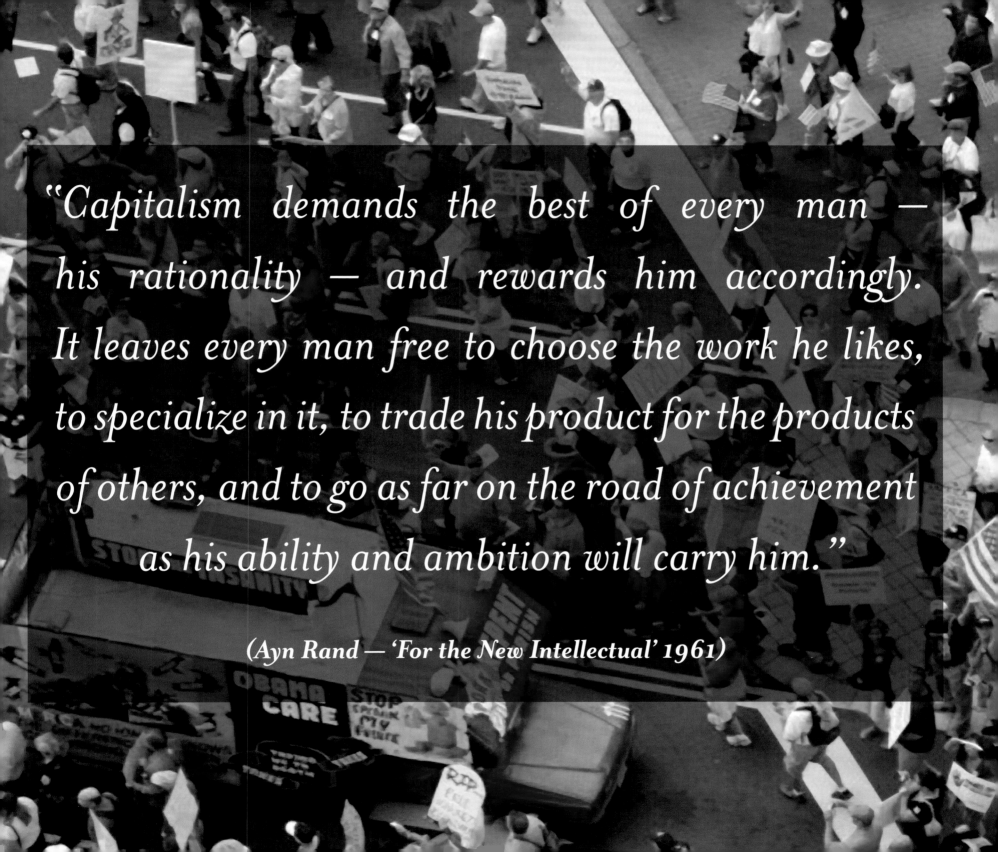

"*Capitalism demands the best of every man — his rationality — and rewards him accordingly. It leaves every man free to choose the work he likes, to specialize in it, to trade his product for the products of others, and to go as far on the road of achievement as his ability and ambition will carry him.*"

(Ayn Rand — 'For the New Intellectual' 1961)

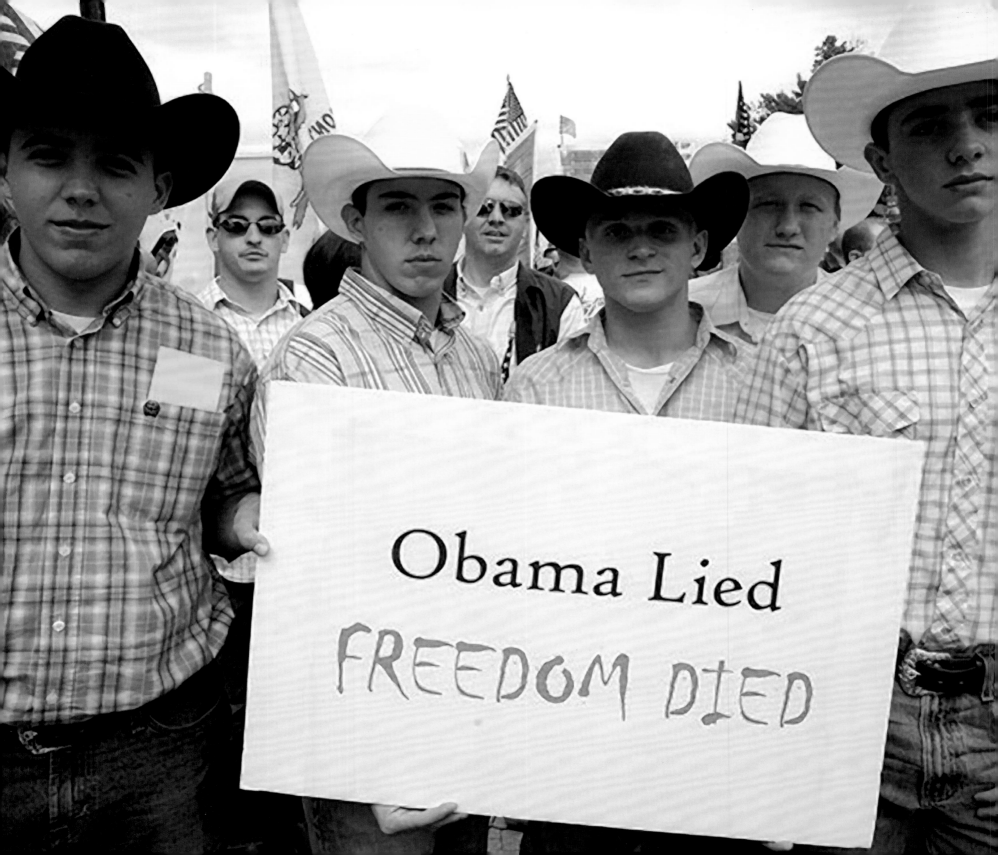

67 YEARS AGO
YOU ASKED HIM TO GIVE
HIS LIFE FOR OUR COUNTRY

NOW YOU WANT HIS LIFE
SO ILLEGALS CAN STILL
GET FREE HEALTH CARE
HE'S NOT EXPENDABLE
HE'S MY DAD!

I've Changed

$37,000
IN DEBT ???
I ONLY MAKE
$10 AWEEK
FOR
ALLOWANCE

A JUST GOVERNMENT PROTECTS
THE INDIVIDUAL'S RIGHTS TO:
LIFE
LIBERTY
PROPERTY
ANYTHING LESS IS A DERELICTION
OF DUTY.
ANYTHING MORE IS AN ABUSE OF
POWER.

REGISTERED
DEMOCRAT
WITH
VOTERS
REMORSE
SORRY
AMERICA

The Greatest
Generation
Did Not Figh
for
Socialism
NOBA

If you think health care is expensive now, wait until it's free.

Mr. President, you are NOT smarter than a 5th grader! Leave the kids alone!

TREAD ON ME

FREEDOM! THEY DIED FOR IT! WHAT'S IT WORTH TO YOU?

NO COMPROMISE
WE DEMAND FREEDOM

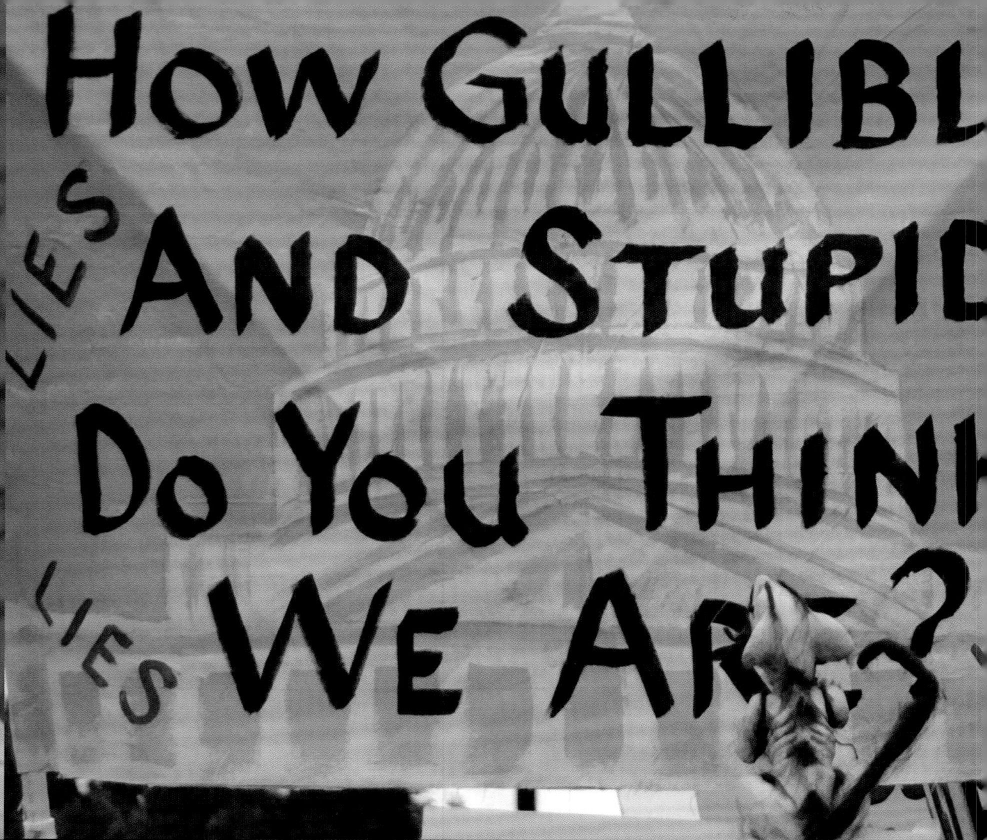

How GULLIBL[E]
LIES AND STUPID
DO YOU THINK
LIES WE ARE?

RESTORE THE
REPUBLIC
REVOLT AGAINST
SOCIALISM

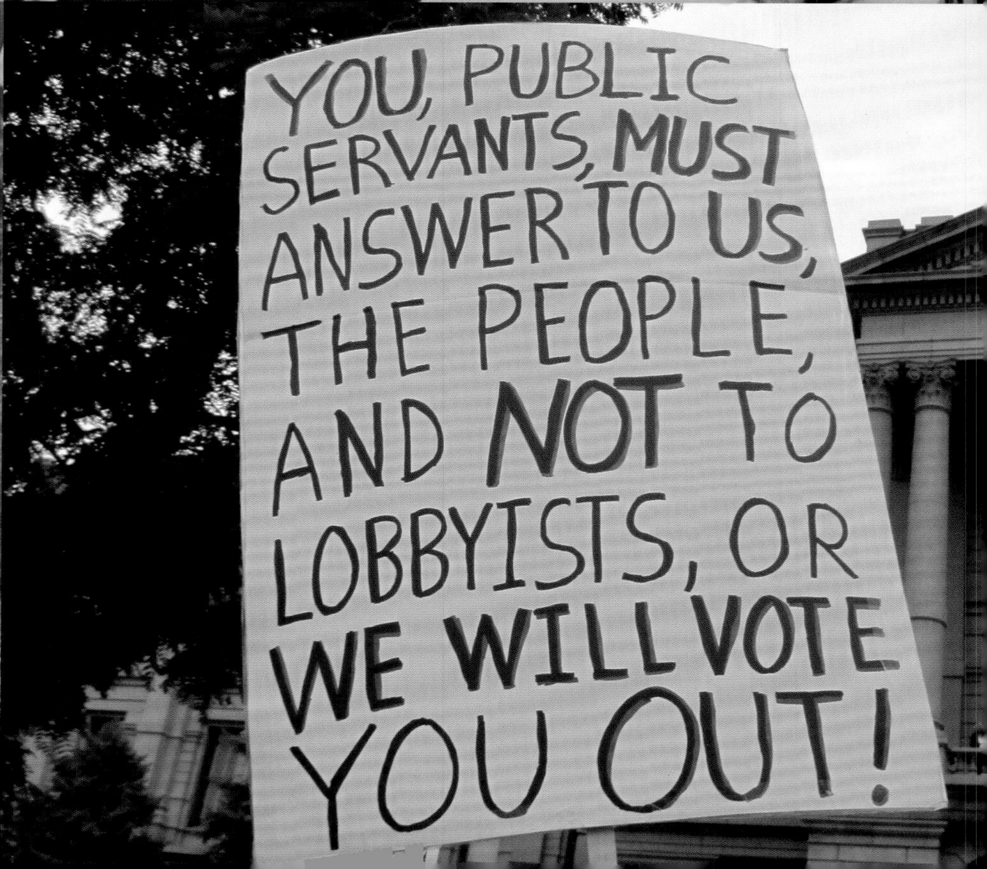

YOU, PUBLIC SERVANTS, MUST ANSWER TO US, THE PEOPLE, AND NOT TO LOBBYISTS, OR WE WILL VOTE YOU OUT!

IT'S NOT ABOUT DEMOCRATS OR REPUBLICANS; IT'S ALL ABOUT OUR FREEDOM AND OUR CONSTITUTION!

DENVER ANTI-TAX TEA PARTY 27 YEAR RETIRED COLONE TO OBAMA, I'M A "DANGEROUS RIGHT WING, RADICAL VET'ERAN"

CONGRESS DON'T UNDERESTIMATE US!

Look Where We are HEADE AMERICA

DOCTORS + NURSES DO NOT SUPPORT OBAMACARE

BROTHER, YOU AIN'T MY KEEPER!

WWW.TIADaily.com

SWORN OATH DEFEND COUNTRY AGAINST ENEMIES FOREIGN AND DOMESTIC WHITEHOUSE FULL OF ENEMI LET'S ROL

POSITIONS TO FILL
535 LEGISLATORS 9 JUDGES
1 PRESIDENT / 1 VP
REQUIREMENTS:
BE ABLE TO READ, BELIEVE IN CAPITALISM & FREEDOM, & SUPPORT/DEFEND CONSTITUTION
Czars/Bureaucrats Need Not Apply

IF YOU THINK YOUR HEALTHCARE IS EXPENSIVE NOW, WAIT UNTIL IT'S FREE

Concentrated Power has always been the enemy of Liberty.
-R Reagan

YOU WANT TO SPEND WHAT? LOL

Obama Care Makes Me SICK!

CAPITALISM Made America Not the Governmen

If you are not scared, you are not paying attention!

+ & +

=

Do the math America!

YOU CAN'T DEBATE WITH LIARS

Liberty

HOW SWEET IT IS

SHOVEL READY HEALTHCARE

OUR TAX DOLLARS FUNDING CORRUPTION AT ACORN!! WHY WON'T CONGRESS ACT?

RIGHT-WING EXTREMISTS

This country was built by the philosophy of equal opportunity, not equal results!

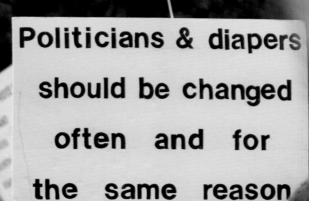

Politicians & diapers should be changed often and for the same reason

NO OBAMACARE

IT'S NOT ABOUT MEDICINE — IT'S ABOUT CONTROL

"I don't have to tell you things are bad. Everybody knows things are bad. It's a depression. Everybody's out of work or scared of losing their job. The dollar buys a nickel's worth; banks are going bust; shopkeepers keep a gun under the counter; punks are running wild in the street and there's nobody anywhere who seems to know what to do, and there's no end to it!

We know the air is unfit to breathe and our food is unfit to eat. And we sit watching our TV's while some local newscaster tells us that today we had fifteen homicides and sixty-three violent crimes, as if that's the way it's supposed to be.

We know things are bad – worse than bad. They're crazy!

It's like everything everywhere is going crazy, so we don't go out anymore. We sit in the house, and slowly the world we're living in is getting smaller, and all we say is, 'Please, at least leave us alone in our living rooms. Let me have my toaster and my TV and my steel-belted radials, and I won't say anything. Just leave us alone!'

Well, I'm not gonna leave you alone. I want you to get mad!

I don't want you to protest. I don't want you to riot – I don't want you to write to your Congressman because I wouldn't know what to tell you to write. I don't know what to do about the depression and the inflation and the Russians and the crime in the street.

All I know is that first, you've got to get mad!"

(Howard Beale, played by Peter Finch, in 'Network' 1976)

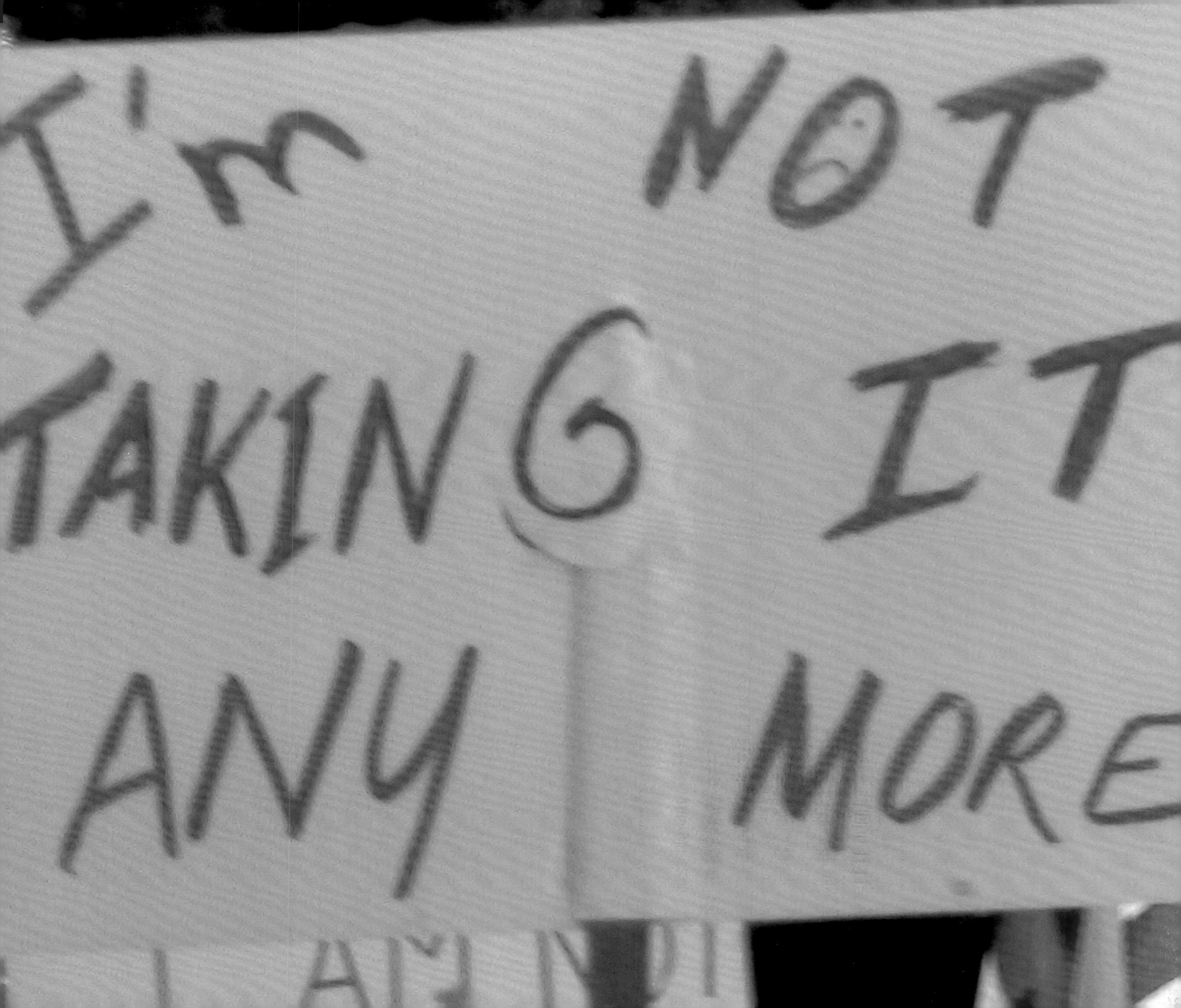

I'm NOT
TAKING IT
ANY MORE

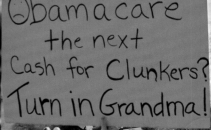

Constitution = Liberty
NOT
NATIONAL
SOCIALISM

NO MORE CASH 4
THESE CLUNKERS

ACORN

I will not shut u^{be}
I will not get ou
of the way

JOE WILSON
TRUTH CZAR

FORT LAUDERDALE FLORIDA
TEAPARTYFTL@GMAIL.COM

HOME LAND
SECURITY
A Citizen
With A Gun

YOU'LL BE
CZARY

OUR PATIENTS
ARE NOT
LIVESTOCK
ON A GOVT RANCH

Leave Terrorists
in GITMO
NOT
USA Standish USA
Michigan !!!!!

Stop Worshipin
Obama!
Get A Job!

This is
our house

SAY NO TO
HEALTH CARE REFORM
WE DON'T NEED MORE
WASTE, FRAUD AND
ABUSE !

GIVE
FREEDOM
A CHANCE

FreeDomWorks.com

WE THE PEOPLE...
SAY NO
TO GOV'T
HEALTHCARE

My Unemployment
Check paid for this sign
Obama Lied... COBRA was
only extended in CA, the bankrupt state!
We don't want your stinking heathcare...
Reform Private insurance to make affordable

MONEY ONLY
GROWS ON
ACORN TREES

OBAMA
the
EXTERMINATOR

illing Our Jobs
illing Our Future
illing Our Freedom

ATLAS
WILL
SHRUG

HANDS
OFF MY
MONEY
GUNS
HEALTHCARE

PARTY LIKE IT'S 1773!

Need Job To Pay TAXES

We the People say...
RESTORE THE REPUBLIC
REVOLT AGAINST SOCIALISM!

MR. GROW UP!
STOP BLAMING
BUSH ET AL

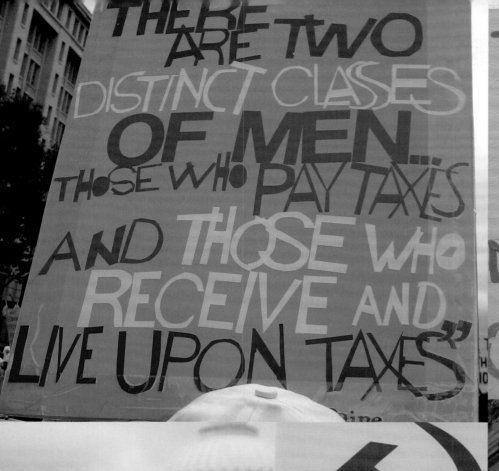

THERE ARE TWO DISTINCT CLASSES OF MEN... THOSE WHO PAY TAXES AND THOSE WHO RECEIVE AND LIVE UPON TAXES"

THE ONLY THING GROWING FASTE THAN THE NATIONAL DEBT IS OBAMA'S NOS

OBAMA'S HELL CARE SENIOR'S PAIN KILLERS

POOP
Prisoners of Obama's Policies

NOT MY COUNTRY!

THE PRESS LOVED MUSSOLINI TOO

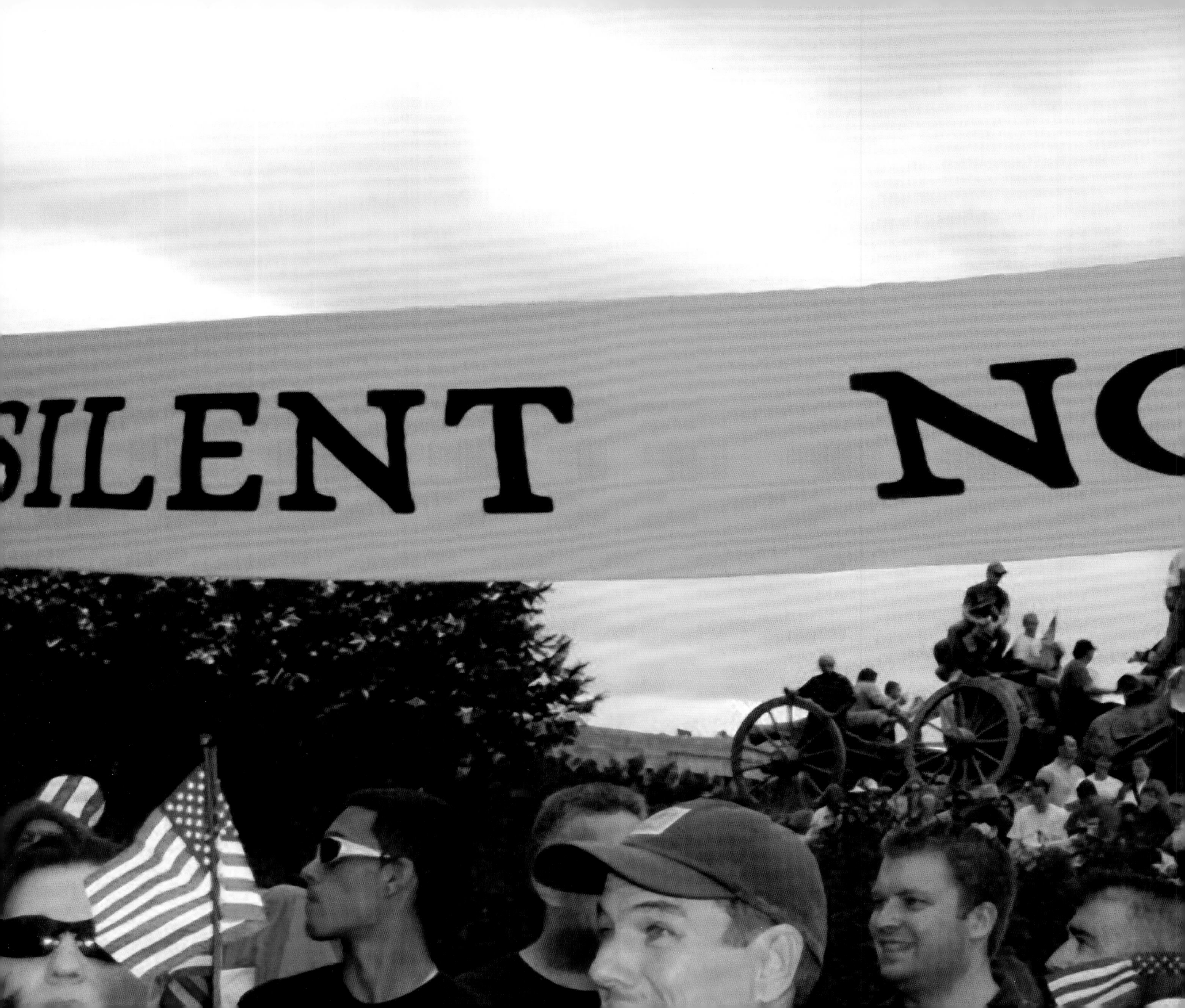
SILENT NO

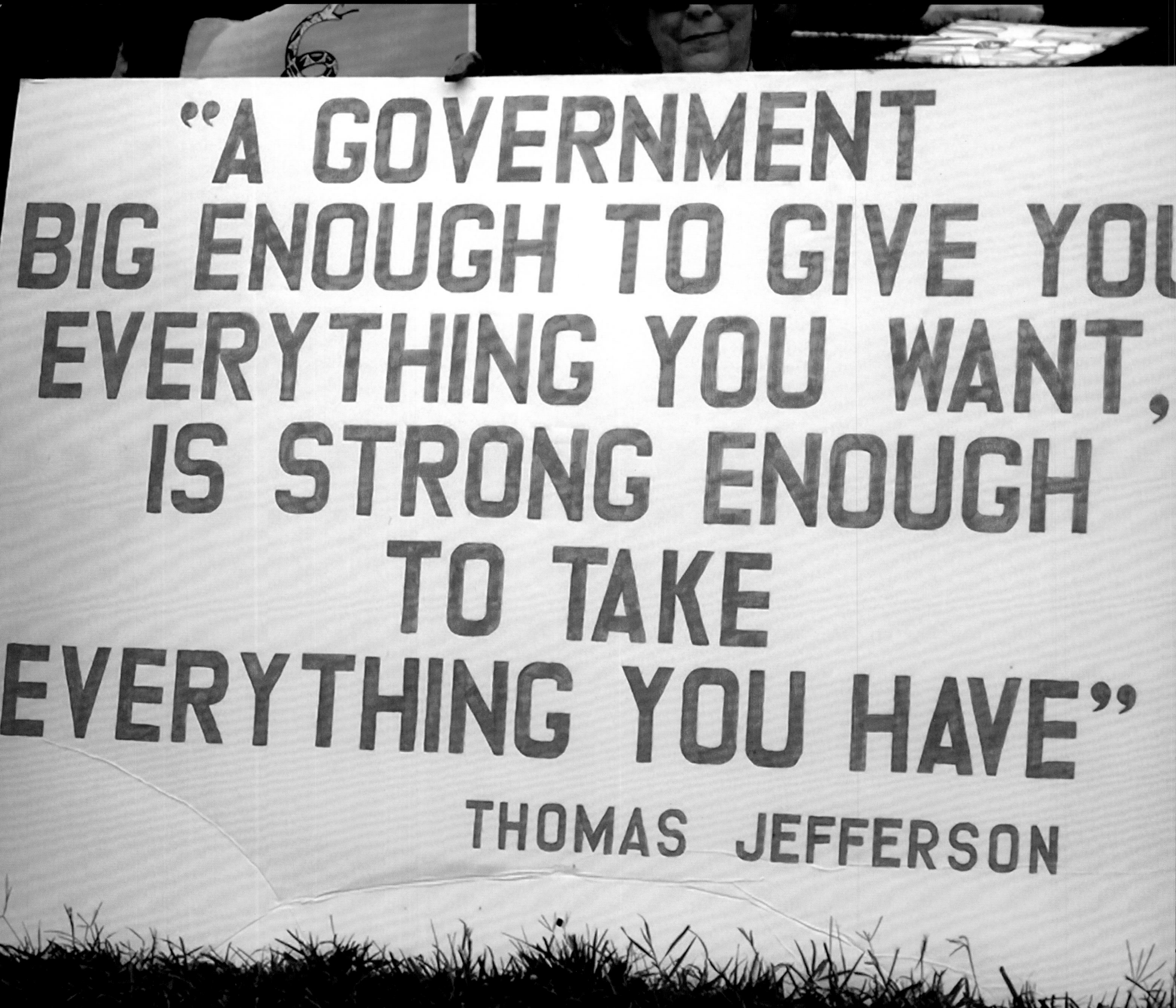
"A GOVERNMENT
BIG ENOUGH TO GIVE YO
EVERYTHING YOU WANT,
IS STRONG ENOUGH
TO TAKE
EVERYTHING YOU HAVE"
THOMAS JEFFERSON

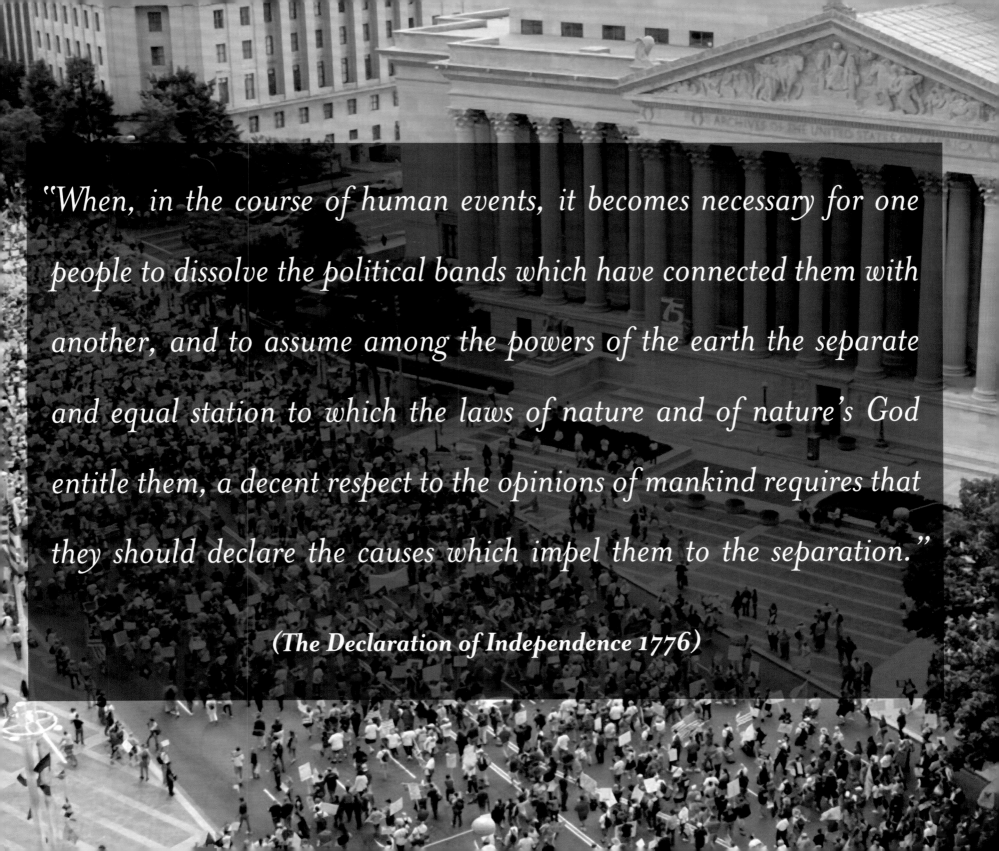

"When, in the course of human events, it becomes necessary for one people to dissolve the political bands which have connected them with another, and to assume among the powers of the earth the separate and equal station to which the laws of nature and of nature's God entitle them, a decent respect to the opinions of mankind requires that they should declare the causes which impel them to the separation."

(The Declaration of Independence 1776)

Photographs taken by:

Andrew Aliferis	Hana Ciembronowicz	Patrick Jennings	Kimberly Orr	Danielle Urschel
Barbara Auchter	Jeff Cruser	William Johns	M. Shoakena	Frank Vest
Mac Bailey	Jerry Douglas	Elizabeth Lynch	Michigan Jay Sunde	Shari Wilcoxon
Barry Bench	Earl Grad	Barbara Kralis	Kelly Swart	David Williams
Brian Carreras	Linda Griggs	Justin Michael	Belinda Szmytke	Dave 'Badmonkey' Willis

Special thanks to:

Jim Fletcher	Eric Kampmann	Matthew Leonard	Ryan Parry	Albert Thompson

Don't Tread on US!

WND Books

Published by WorldNetDaily

Los Angeles, CA

Copyright © 2010 by Mark Karis

"Foreword" Copyright © 2010 by Chuck Norris

Book designed by Mark Karis

Cover photographed by Pete Duval

WND Books are distributed to the trade by:

Midpoint Trade Books

27 West 20th Street, Suite 1102

New York, NY 10011

WND Books are available at special discounts for bulk purchases.

WND Books, Inc. also publishes books in electronic formats.

For more information call (310) 961-4170 or visit www.wndbooks.com.

First Edition

ISBN 10-Digit: 1935071866

ISBN 13-Digit: 9781935071860

Library of Congress information is available upon request

www.DontTreadOnUS.com

Printed in Italy

10 9 8 7 6 5 4 3 2 1

Standing up for what you believe is hard when you're outnumbered.

A badge of courage can give you the spirit you need to make sure others

hear your voice loud and clear. Make a bold statement this year —

and every year — with one of the newest additions to our line of

BUMPER STICKERS, SIGNS, T-SHIRTS, BANNERS, FLAGS, PINS, *and more!*

    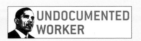